HIMALAYAN
RIVERS, LAKES AND GLACIERS

HIMALAYAN RIVERS, LAKES AND GLACIERS

S.S. NEGI
Divisional Forest Officer
H.P. Forest Training School
Chail, Himachal Pradesh

INDUS PUBLISHING COMPANY
NEW DELHI

Geology
GB
1359
.H54
N44
1991

© 1991 S.S. Negi

First published in 1991 by
Indus Publishing Company
FS-5, Tagore Garden, New Delhi 110027

ISBN 81-85182-61-2

Published by M.L. Gidwani, Indus Publishing Company
FS-5, Tagore Garden, New Delhi 110027, and printed at
Elegant Printers, New Delhi 110064

Preface

Stretching from the great bend of the Indus river in the north-west to the bend of the Brahmaputra river in the east, the Himalayan mountain chain is a gigantic measuring rod on the face of the earth. Its snow-clad peaks tower to elevations of over 8000 metres. Geo-politically speaking the Himalaya encompasses Jammu and Kashmir, Himachal Pradesh, Garhwal, Kumaun, Nepal, Darjeeling hills, Sikkim, Bhutan and Arunachal Pradesh west of the Brahmaputra river.

This mountain chain has aptly been described as the world's most magnificent physical feature. The Himalayan mountain wall is made up of countless mountain peaks, valleys, glaciers, lakes, rivers and streams. Some of the most important rivers of the south-east Asia drain the Himalaya. These include Indus, Ganga and Brahmaputra. Some of the beautiful lakes like the Dal lake and Nainital lake lie in the Himalaya. The world's largest glacier (outside the poles) the Siachen glacier too lies in the trans-Himalayan Karakoram range.

Hundreds of rivers, lakes and glaciers of this mountain chain have fascinated the sages, poets, scientists and even the common man since times immemorial. The need for a comprehensive book of these physical features was being felt for a very long time. The present book attempts to fulfil this gap and aims at placing the scattered knowledge and information at one place, so that the seekers of knowledge and information can have easy access to the material. It describes in brief all the rivers, lakes and glaciers of the Himalaya and will aptly serve the needs of the environmentalists, engineers, scientists, tourists and even the laymen interested to know about Himalayan rivers, lakes and glaciers.

My extensive travels in the Himalaya as a geologist have proved to be a handy tool during the preparation of this book.

I am thankful to my friends, colleagues and well-wishers for their constant encouragement in my endeavour. Thanks are due to Manju for her patience and to the publishers for mooting this idea and bringing out this book in a short time.

S.S. Negi

Contents

PREFACE	5
PHYSICAL SET UP OF THE HIMALAYA	9
RIVERS	31
LAKES	144
GLACIERS	158

Physical Set up of the Himalaya

The Himalaya are the most magnificent feature on the face of the earth. They form a part of a complex of folded mountain chains that radiate from the Pamir Knot in Iran. The others are the Kun-Lun, Sayan, Lin Shan, Toros, Elburz, Dinarska, Pyrenes and the Tein Shan mountains. The Indus gap at the base of the Nanga Parbat in the north-west and the Brahmaputra gap at the foot of the Namche Barwa peak in the east are two extreme ends of the Himalaya. Between these two limits there occurs a complex system of high mountains, deep river valleys, gurgling streams and flat alluvial terraces. Countless rivers, streams and rivulets drain this mountain system.

Physiographic Divisions

The Himalaya may aptly be divided into four distinct physiographic divisions from south to north.

1. *Siwalik Hills*

This is a series of low hills aligned more or less parallel to the main Himalayan arc. The Siwalik hills are very well developed in the western and central Himalaya, east of which they gradually merge with the lower Himalayan foothills. The highest peaks of the Siwalik system rise to elevations of over 1000 metres.

Longitudinal valleys separate the Siwalik hills in the south from the lower Himalaya in the north. These are known as dun valleys, e.g., Kiarda dun, Dehradun and Patli dun valleys.

2. *Lower Himalaya*

This consists of the foothills or lower hills of the main Himalayan range that lies further towards north. In many areas the lower Himalaya rise abruptly above the dun type valleys. The highest mountain peaks in the lower Himalaya tower to an elevation of over 3300 metres.

3. *Higher Himalaya*

This consists of the main Himalayan mountain wall that extends in an arcuate shape along the periphery of the Indian sub-continent. Some of the highest mountain peaks in the world are a part of the main Himalaya, viz Everest, Makalu and Kanchanjunga.

4. *Trans-Himalaya*

Across the soaring, snow-clad peaks of the main Himalaya lies a vast tableland having an average elevation of over 3000 metres. Conditions are akin to those prevailing in Tibet and hence this region has also been termed as the Tibetan Himalaya. This is primarily a rain-deficient area as the SW monsoons are unable to cross the main Himalayan barrier that lies to the south of this tract. Thus conditions resemble a desert and the trans-Himalaya has often been described as a cold desert.

Regional Set Up

The Himalaya is made up of a number of geo-political regions. The physical set up of each of these regions has been described in the following text (from west to east).

Jammu and Kashmir

The state of Jammu and Kashmir is a part of the Union of India. It is made up of the following physical units--

a) *Karakoram range*: This snow-clad mountain range lies to the north of the main Himalaya and Zaskar ranges in the Ladakh region of Jammu and Kashmir. More than ten peaks have an elevation of over 7000 metres. These include K2, Gasherbrum, Dast-i-Ghil Sar, Terem Kangri, Rakaposhi, Sasser Kangri and the Golden Throne. The Karakoram range forms a part of the trans-Himalaya. Its average elevation is over 3000 metres.

The Karakoram range has some of the highest glaciers in the world. Prominent amongst these is the Siachen glacier which has a length of about 72 kms.

b) *Gilgit valley*: This is a fertile valley lying in the north-western part of Jammu and Kashmir. It is surrounded by high mountain peaks having an elevation of over 7000 metres. The Gilgit valley opens into the Indus valley near Bunji at an elevation of about 1400 metres.

c) *Ladakh plateau*: The Ladakh plateau lies to the north of the main Himalaya. It has an average elevation of over 3500 metres.

There are a number of prominent river valleys that drain into the Indus river or into the many salt-encrusted lakes in eastern Ladakh, e.g., Salt lake. The Soda plains and Aksai Chin are some of the main physical features of the Ladakh plateau.

d) *Zaskar range*: This is another trans-Himalayan range of the Ladakh region. It is a desolate tract made up of high mountains, river valleys and glaciers. The eastern part of this range is known as Rupshu in which occurs the famous salt encrusted lake of Tso-Morari.

e) *Great Himalaya*: The great Himalayan range branches off from the Nanga Parbat massif and runs along an arc passing to the north of the Kashmir valley and south of the Zaskar range towards south-east into Himachal Pradesh. There are a number of high passes across these mountains, viz Burzil La and Zoji La.

f) *Kashmir valley*: The broad open valley of Kashmir lies between the main or great Himalayan range in the north and the Pir Panjal in the south. The Kashmir valley is drained by the river Jhelum which winds its way across this valley. Its tributaries are Liddar and Sind.

A vast lake covered this valley in the past. It was formed when the rising Pir Panjal range blocked the flow of the Jhelum river. The lake bottom was exposed once the natural dam burst. The Wular, Dal and Nagin lakes are remnants of this water-body.

g) *Pir Panjal range*: This mountain range runs in an arc shape along the southern periphery of the Kashmir valley. Its peaks rise to an elevation of about 3000 to 4000 metres. The Pir Panjal range has been cut across by the river Jhelum near Baramula and the river Chenab below Kistwar.

h) *Siwalik hills*: These are low hills running more or less parallel to the lower Himalayan or Pir Panjal range. They merge with the Siwalik hills of Himachal Pradesh in the east.

Himachal Pradesh

The state of Himachal Pradesh is a part of the Union of India. It is made up of the following physical units—

a) *Lahul and Spiti valleys*: These are two distinct valleys lying in the trans-Himalayan tract of Himachal Pradesh. The Lahul valley is drained by the rivers Chandra and Bhaga which join to form the Chenab. The Spiti valley is drained by the Spiti river. This area is a rain-deficient cold desert.

b) *Great Himalaya*: The great or main Himalayan range runs in an arc shape along the northern part of the state. It is comprised of snow-clad peaks, glaciers and deep valleys. This range has been cut by the rivers Chenab and Satluj.

c) *Dhauladhar range*: The Dhauladhar range rises abruptly above the Kangra valley and the plains of Punjab. Its upper tracts are under a permanent cover of snow. The river Beas has cut across this range at Larji. Further towards east, the Dhauladhar range gives way to a series of mountain ranges of the lower Himalaya. These are the Nag Tibba range, the Shimla hills and the Churdhar ridge.

d) *Kulu valley*: This is a broad valley formed by the river Beas. It is bound in the north by the main Himalayan range and on other sides by the Dhauladhar and an extension of the Pir Panjal range.

e) *Lower Himalaya*: The lower Himalayan range of Himachal Pradesh is an eastern extension of the Dhauladhar range. Churdhar peak on the border of Sirmour and Shimla districts is the highest point of this range.

f) *Siwalik hills*:The Siwalik hills are prominently developed all along the southern periphery of Himachal Pradesh. These hills are extensive in Kangra, Hamirpur, Una, Mandi, Bilaspur, Solan and Sirmour districts. In Paonta area, a dun type valley known as the Kiarda dun has developed between the lower Himalaya in the north and the Siwalik hills in the south.

Garhwal and Kumaun

The eight districts of Uttarkashi, Chamoli, Pauri, Tehri, Dehradun, Almora, Pithoragarh and Nainital constitute Garhwal and Kumaon and are a part of Uttar Pradesh. They may be divided into the following physical units—

a) *Yamuna valley*: The river Yamuna rises from the snowy wastes at the base of the Bandarpunch peak in Uttarkashi district. It is a V-shaped valley and the river winds past terraces and gorges before entering the plains near Dehradun.

b) *Bhagirathi valley*: The Bhagirathi river rises from the Gangotri glacier at the base of the Bandarpunch peak. It flows across the lower Himalayan mountain range to merge with the Alaknanda at Deoparyag, downstream of which the river is known as the Ganga.

c) *Alaknanda valley*: The Alaknanda river rises from the base of the Chaukhamba peak. It flows across the lower Himalayan mountain ranges to merge with the Bhagirathi at Deoparyag.

d) *Great Himalaya*: The great or main Himalayan range occurs in the form of a gigantic wall of ice, bare rock and rugged peaks. It runs along the northern periphery of Garhwal and Kumaun. All major rivers of this region originate from the snowy wastes occurring at the base of the great Himalayan mountain range.

e) *Lower Himalaya*: This is comprised of a series of mountain ranges that lie to the south of the main or great Himalayan range. Different names have been given to the lower Himalaya in various tracts—
 — Nag Tibba ridge in Chakrata area
 — Mussoorie ridge in Mussoorie area
 — Nainital ridge in Nainital area.

f) *Siwalik hills*: The Siwalik hills are very well developed in Garhwal and Kumaun. They occupy a position which is more or less parallel to the lower Himalaya. The tops of these hills rise to elevations of over 3000 metres.

g) *Dun valleys*: Longitudinal valleys are located between the Siwalik hills in the south and the lower Himalaya in the north, viz Dehradun valley.

Nepal

Nepal is an independent country in the central Himalaya. It is divided into the following physical units—

a) *Mustang-Bhot region*: This is a trans-Himalayan tract in north-central Nepal. This is largely an arid to semi-arid area receiving very low rainfall.

b) *Great Himalaya*: The great Himalaya extends in an arcuate shape along the northern boundary of Nepal. They extend from the Api and Nampa peaks in the west to the Kanchanjunga peak in the east along the border of Nepal and Sikkim. This mountain range also includes Mount Everest, the highest peak in the world. The main Himalayan mountain range has been cut across by a number of rivers originating in the trans-Himalayan zone.

Leban (1972) has sub-divided the main Himalaya of Nepal into the following sub-units—
 — Western high Himalaya
 — Arid high Himalaya
 — Central high Himalaya
 — Eastern high Himalaya.

c) *Lower or middle Himalaya*: These are a series of mountain ranges occurring to the south of the great or main Himalaya. The highest peaks of these mountains tower to elevations of over 3300 metres. Spectacular gorges have been cut by the main rivers of Nepal which flow in a general direction towards the plains of India.

Amongst the mountain ranges which constitute the lower or middle Himalaya are—
- Humla-Jumla mountains
- Baitadi mountains
- Dailekh mountains
- Piuthan mountains
- Baglung mountains
- Mahabharat Lekh

Leban (1972) has referred to these mountains as the 'midlands' and 'transitional' mountains.

d) *Kathmandu valley*: This is a circular basin drained by the Bagmati river and its tributaries in central Nepal. It is believed that the entire valley was covered by a vast lake in the geological past. This lake was formed as the rising Himalaya blocked the flow of the Bagmati river. Later on, this natural dam burst and the Kathmandu valley was exposed. This valley is hemmed on all sides by high mountains.

e) *Siwalik hills*: The low rolling Siwalik hills are the southernmost mountain range of Nepal. These hills lie more or less parallel to the main Himalayan mountain wall. Their tops have an elevation of about 1000 metres.

f) *Dun valleys*: A number of longitudinal valleys occur between the Siwalik hills in the south and the lower or middle Himalaya in the north. These valleys are the Bhitri Madhesh, Kamla, Narayni, Chitwan and Rapti dun valleys.

Sikkim and Darjeeling Hills

Sikkim is a separate state within the Union of India, while the Darjeeling hills are a part of the Indian state of West Bengal. They may be divided into the following physical units—

a) *Great Himalaya*: The great or main Himalayan range runs all along the northern border of Sikkim between the Kanchanjunga massif in the west and the Chomolhari in the east. It comprises of a number of peaks having an elevation of over 7000 metres.

The Singalila in the west and the Dongkya in the east are two transverse north-south mountain ranges arising from the main Himalayan mountain wall. These include high snow-clad mountain peaks soaring to altitudes of over 6000 metres.

A number of glaciers descend from the main Himalaya and its offshoots. The largest is the Zemu glacier from the snout of which rises the Teesta river.

b) *Lower Himalaya or Darjeeling hills*: The lower Himalaya is made up of the Gangtok ridge in Sikkim and the Darjeeling hills. The latter are divided into two by the deep gorge of the Teesta river. To the east of this gorge lie the Kalimpong hills with mountain peaks rising to over 3000 metres. Rivers radiate in all directions from these hills and flow into the Teesta river.

The Tiger hill is the highest peak in the Darjeeling hills. Spurs radiate from it in all directions. Amongst these are—
-- Darjeeling ridge to the north
-- Tadah spur to the east
-- Dow hill ridge to the south
-- Ghoom ridge to the west.

c) *Foothills*: Low rolling hills represent the foothills of the Sikkim-Darjeeling region. The foothills are not as well developed as the Siwalik hills of the western and central Himalaya and tend to merge with the lower Himalayan ranges.

Bhutan

Bhutan is an independent country lying in the eastern Himalaya. It may be divided into the following physical units—

a) *Great Himalaya*: The main or great Himalayan range of Bhutan runs along its northern border from the Chomolhari peak in the west to the Kulha Kangri peak in the east. Further towards east this mountain wall extends into Arunachal Pradesh.

The great Himalayan range includes many high mountain peaks. Its southern slopes are glaciated. There occur a number of glacial basins, lakes, moraines and amphitheatres from which arise numerous rivers and streams.

b) *River valleys*: There are no large river basins in Bhutan. The largest river is the Manas in the east that flows into the Brahmaputra river. In the west, the Amo Chu river enters Bhutan from Chumbi valley through a deep gorge. It flows towards south to enter the plains near Jalpaiguri.

c) *Lower Himalaya*: The middle or lower Himalaya of Bhutan consist of a series of mountain ranges that run more or less parallel to the great Himalayan mountain wall. This range rises abruptly above the plains or the foothills. The peaks may rise to an elevation of over 3500 metres.

d) *Foothills*: The foothills of Bhutan are not very extensively developed. They are a series of low hills extending all along the southern periphery of the country.

Arunachal Pradesh

Arunachal Pradesh is a state within the Union of India. It occupies the easternmost part of the Himalaya. Only that part of this state which lies to the west of the Brahmaputra river is included in the Himalaya. Thus the Lohit and Dihang catchments of Arunachal Pradesh are not a part of the Himalaya. This state may be divided into the following physical units—

a) *Great Himalaya*: The main or great Himalaya runs all along the northern border of this state upto the Namche Barwa peak that marks the eastern extremity of the Himalaya. High, snow-clad peaks and glaciers form a part of the main Himalayan mountain wall.

b) *Lower Himalaya*: The lower or middle Himalaya of Arunachal Pradesh is made up of a few parallel ranges lying to the south of the great Himalayan range. Many of these ranges rise abruptly above the plains. Rivers and streams have cut deep gorges across the lower Himalaya.

c) *Foothills*: The foothills of Arunachal Pradesh are not as well formed as the Siwalik hills of western and central Himalaya. They consist of a number of mountains of height upto about 1000 metres lying more or less parallel to the great and lower Himalayan ranges in the north. These foothills gradually merge with the Brahmaputra plains in the south.

Climate

The climatic conditions of the Himalaya are extremely varied in nature. There is a marked change in the climate from the wettest spots of Arunachal Pradesh to the cold deserts of Ladakh and Lahul.

On the basis of altitude, the Himalaya may be divided into the following climatic regions (after Negi 1982 and 1990):

Climatic region	*Altitudinal range (in metres)*
Western Himalaya	
Arctic	Over 4500
Sub-arctic	3500 to 4500

Temperate	2000 to 3500
Sub-tropical	700 to 2000
Tropical	below 700

Central Himalaya

Arctic	Over 5500
Sub-arctic	4500 to 5500
Cold temperate	3500 to 4500
Cool temperate	2000 to 3500
Warm sub-tropical	700 to 2000
Warm tropical	below 700

Eastern Himalaya

Arctic	Over 6000
Sub-arctic	4800 to 6000
Cold temperate	3800 to 4800
Cool temperate	2200 to 3800
Warm sub-tropical	800 to 2200
Warm tropical	below 800

Cycle of Seasons

It becomes warm in most parts of the Himalaya in May and June. Snow melts at a very fast rate in this season and hence the water level in the rivers is quite high. Monsoon rains start from late June to September. Very heavy rains are received on the south-facing slopes of the Himalaya. Very sparse rains occur in the trans-Himalayan tract which lies in the rain shadow of the main Himalaya.

The weather clears up in most parts of the Himalaya in October. Winter sets in by late November. In this season precipitation occurs in the form of rain in the lower hills and as snow in the upper tracts. Snow may remain on the ground for several weeks at a stretch during the winter season. Winter ends in mid-March.

The spring season is short. It extends from mid-March to late April after which the summer season sets in.

Gravity winds are a very common feature in most parts of the Himalaya. At sunset due to changes in temperature and pressure conditions, there is a downward wind which takes with it cloud and mist into the valley. During the monsoons, it is common to catch sight of a cloud being rolled down into the valley towards evening. At day break and during early part of the day there is a reverse wind flowing from the valley to the top of the hills. Due to the warming effect of the sun, the mist warms up and ascends in altitude. These winds may attain very high speeds.

Natural Vegetation/Forests

Chiefly due to vast changes in climate, altitudinal and aspect conditions that prevail in different parts of the Himalaya, different forest types are found. The principal vegetation/forest groups and types in the Himalaya are (after Champion and Seth 1964 and Negi 1990):

Sub-tropical Semi-desert

This type is found in the hot, dry tracts of the lower hills of Jammu. It is also found in the foothill areas of Himachal Pradesh. It consists of scrub type of forests. The main species are—*Acacia catechu, Bombax ceiba, Dalbergia sissoo, Prosopis spicigera* and *Zizyphus jujuba*.

Sal Forests

Sal forests are found in the lower Himalaya and the foothills from Arunachal Pradesh in the east to Paonta in the west. Different types and sub-types of Sal forests are—
-- Siwalik Sal forest
-- Dry sal forest
-- Terai and bhabar sal forest
-- Dun sal forest
-- Lower Siwalik sal forest.

Montane Sub-tropical Forests

These forests occur in the sub-tropical zone of the Siwalik and lower Himalaya. The following forest types fall within this group—
-- East Himalayan sub-tropical wet hill forest
-- Siwalik chir pine forest
-- Lower Himalayan chir pine forest
-- Sub-tropical dry evergreen forest
-- Sub-tropical riverine forest
-- Sub-tropical wet evergreen forest.

Montane Wet Temperate Forests

These forests are found in the lower temperate zone of the eastern Himalaya usually between an elevation of 1800 metres and 3000

metres. The following forest types fall within this group—
-- East Himalayan semi-evergreen forest
-- East Himalayan wet temperate forest
-- High level oak forest
-- Lauraceous forest.

Himalayan Moist Temperate Forests
This group is well distributed all over the temperate zone of the Himalaya usually between an elevation of 1500 metres and 3300 metres. The following forest types fall within this group—
-- Ban oak forest
-- Moru oak forest
-- Moist deodar forest
-- Moist mixed coniferous forest
-- Moist blue pine forest
-- Kharsu oak forest
-- High level fir and spruce forest
-- Western Himalayan upper oak fir forest
-- East Himalayan mixed coniferous forest
-- East Himalayan mixed temperate forest
-- *Abies delavayi* forest.

Himalayan Dry Temperate Forests
This group occurs mainly in the higher and trans-Himalayan tracts where there is little precipitation in the form of snow. The following forest types form a part of this group—
-- Dry broad-leaved and coniferous forest
-- Neoza or Chilgoza pine forest
-- Dry deodar forest
-- West Himalayan dry temperate forest
-- West Himalayan high level dry blue pine forest
-- West Himalayan dry juniper forest
-- East Himalayan dry temperate coniferous forest
-- East Himalayan dry juniper forest.

Sub-alpine Forests
These are the highest tree forests in the Himalayan region above which no tree forests grow. They occupy an altitudinal position between the temperate forests and alpine meadows. Snow remains on the ground for several weeks at a stretch in this tract. The following

types fall within this group—
- West Himalayan sub-alpine birch/fir forest
- Sub-alpine fir and spruce forest
- Sub-alpine rhododendron forest
- East Himalayan sub-alpine birch/fir forest.

Moist Alpine Scrub

These scrub forests lie just below the snowline, usually above an elevation of 3500 metres. Snow remains on the ground for several weeks at a stretch during the winter season. The total growing period available to the plants is very short. Tree species are stunted and are in the form of shrubs. The following forest types fall within this group—
- Birch-Rhododendron scrub forest
- Deciduous alpine scrub
- Alpine pastures.

Dry Alpine Scrub

Dry alpine scrub is found near the snowline in the inner dry valleys of the higher Himalayan and the trans-Himalayan tracts. Tree growth is virtually absent. Grasses come up in the short growing period that extends from mid-May to late October. Heavy snowfall is received in winter and snow covers the ground for several weeks at a stretch. Vegetation may be semi-xerophytic in nature.

Drainage

The drainage system of the Himalaya is very complex. It consists of rivers, lakes and glaciers. While most of the glaciers are restricted to areas above the tree line, Himalayan rivers criss-cross the entire mountain chain. In fact, a number of rivers are older than the mountain system itself. These include the Indus, Satluj and Brahmaputra. They originate in southern Tibet and have cut across the main Himalayan mountain wall.

Describing this feature Wadia (1975) states, "During the slow process of mountain formation these old rivers kept very much to their own channels . . . . . The great momentum acquired by this upheaval was expanded in eroding their channels at a faster rate. Thus, the elevation of the mountains and the erosion of the valleys proceeding *pari passu* the mountains emerged with a complete valley system cutting it in very deep gorges."

Lakes are found all over the Himalaya. They serve both as inland drainage basins and as a temporary basin for flowing water.

There are three major river systems that drain the Himalaya, viz the Indus system, the Ganga system and the Brahmaputra system.

Indus River System

The Indus river rises from near the lake Mansarovar on the Tibetan plateau and enters the Himalaya in Ladakh. Thereafter it flows through the Ladakh region of Jammu and Kashmir before entering the plains of Pakistan. The main tributaries of the Indus river in Ladakh are--
-- the Shyok river rises in the Despang plains
-- the Shigar river originates from the glaciers on the southern face of the Karakoram range
-- the Gilgit river rises near the north-western boundary of the Himalaya
-- the Astor river rises near the Burzil pass
-- the Shigar (south) river drains the northern slopes of the Himadri
-- the Zaskar river originates from the north-facing slopes of the great Himalaya
-- the Hanle river is a short left bank tributary of the Indus river.

Besides the above tributaries, other important tributaries of the Indus system drain the western Himalaya. These are--

a) *Jhelum*: The Jhelum river rises from the northern slopes of the Pir Panjal range. It drains the Kashmir valley before cutting a deep gorge through the Pir Panjal range near Baramula. Its major tributaries are--
-- the Liddar river originates in the snowy wastes at Chandanwari near the mountain resort of Pahalgam
-- the river Sind originates on the southern slopes of the great Himalayan range that hems the Kashmir valley. It flows into the Jhelum river near Srinagar
-- the river Kishenganga also originates on the south-facing slopes of the great Himalayan range.

b) *Chenab*: The river Chenab is another major tributary of the river Indus. It rises from the Lahul valley of Himachal Pradesh and enters Kishtwar after flowing through the Pangi valley of Himachal Pradesh. Thereafter it flows along the base of the Pir Panjal range and enters the plains.

c) *Ravi*: The Ravi river is the third of the five major tributaries of the Indus river. It originates in the Bara Banghal tract between the Dhauladhar range in the south and the Pir Panjal in the north. This river flows in a more or less westerly direction before it cuts across the Dhauladhar range downstream of which it flows towards southeast to enter the plains of Punjab.

d) *Beas*: The river Beas is another important tributary of the river Indus. It rises from the snowy wastes on the south-facing slopes of the Pir Panjal range near the famous Rohtang pass. It drains past the famous holiday resort of Manali and through the Kulu valley south of which it has cut across the Dhauladhar range at Larji. The main tributaries of the Beas river are—
-- the Parbati river joins the Beas river near Shamshi
-- the Harla river joins the Beas near Bhuntar
-- the Sainj river joins the Beas near Larji
-- the Tirthan river rises in the snows of an offshoot of the Pir Panjal range. It joins the Beas near Larji
-- the tributaries rising from the Dhauladhar range which flow into the Beas river are Uhl, Suketi, Luni, Awa, Banganga, Gaj and Chaki.

The river enters the plains of Punjab near Pathankot after cutting a gorge across the Siwalik range.

e) *Satluj*: The Satluj river rises from near the lake Mansarovar in southern Tibet. It enters India (Himachal Pradesh) near Shipki La. Thereafter it flows through the trans-Himalayan areas of Himachal Pradesh. It cuts a spectacular gorge across the main Himalaya, flows at the base of the Shimla ridge and enters the plains of Punjab downstream of the Bhakra dam.

The main tributaries of the Satluj are the rivers Spiti and Baspa.

Ganga River System

The Ganga river system drains a major part of the Himalaya, from the south-eastern slopes of the Shimla ridge to eastern Nepal. There are a number of tributaries of the Ganga river system. These are—

a) *Yamuna*: The Yamuna river is the largest tributary of the Ganga river. It drains the westernmost part of the Ganga catchment. The main tributaries of the Yamuna river are—
-- the Tons river rises in the snows beyond the high altitude valley of Har-ki-dun

- the river Aglar flows along the base of the northern slopes of the Mussoorie ridge
- the Giri river drains the south-eastern corner of Himachal Pradesh
- the Bata river originates on the lower slopes of the Nahan ridge and drains the Paonta valley.

b) *Bhagirathi*: The Bhagirathi is one of the two rivers that merge to form the Ganga river at Deoparyag. It rises from the snout of the Gangotri glacier at the base of the Chaukhamba massif. It is joined by the Alaknanda at Deoparyag, downstream of which the channel is known as the Ganga river.

Important tributaries of the Bhagirathi river are--
- the Janhvi river that flows into the Bhagirathi near Uttarkashi
- the Bhilangana river which flows into the Bhagirathi near Tehri.

c) *Alaknanda*: The river Alaknanda and its tributaries drain the central part of the U.P. Himalaya. It rises from the snowy wastes to the north of Badrinath and merges with the Bhagirathi river at Deoparyag. Main tributaries of the Alaknanda river are--
- the Mandakini river rises from the snows to the north-east of Kedarnath. It joins the Alaknanda at Rudraparyag
- the Pindar river rises from the Pindari glacier on the south-western slopes of the Alaknanda-Kali water-divide. It merges with the Alaknanda at Karanparyag
- the Nandakini river is another important tributary of the Alaknanda. It joins the main river at Nandparyag
- the river Dhauliganga rises from the snowy wastes on the southern face of the main Himalayan range.

d) *Kali*: The Kali river forms the border between India and Nepal. It flows in a more or less SSW direction along a narrow V-shaped valley. The main tributaries of this river are--
- the Kalapani river is the eastern headwaters of the Kali river
- the Kuthi Yankti river is the western headwaters of the Kali river. It rises on the southern slopes of the main Himalaya
- the Goriganga river rises from the snow-bound slopes of the Alaknanda-Kali water-divide
- the Sarju river is another important tributary of the Kali river. It drains west-central Kumaun
- the Ladhiya river rises from a number of spring-fed streams in the south-eastern corner of Kumaun.

The Kali river enters the plains at Baramdeo and it is known as the river Sarda.

e) *Ghagra*: This river system drains western Nepal. Its main tributaries are--
- the Karnali river is the largest river draining into the river Ghagra. It has cut a deep gorge across the main or great Himalayan range
- the Seti river rises near Api. It flows in an easterly direction to join the Karnali
- the Bheri river rises in the snows of the Dhaulagiri massif. Its waters drain into the mainstream in the lower hills of Nepal.

The combined Ghagra river pierces the lower hills near Gaindakanda to enter the plains of Bihar.

f) *Gandak*: The Gandak river system drains central Nepal. It joins the river Ganga in the plains. Its main tributaries are--
- the Kali or Krishna Gandaki river is the most important tributary of this river system. It rises in the trans-Himalaya
- the Seti Gandak river rises from the base of the Annapurna Himal massif
- the Marsyandi river flows between the Annapurna Himal and the Manaslu
- the Trisuli river rises from the Ganesh Himal.

The combined Gandak river has cut across the lower hills. It flows through the thickly forested Chitwan valley to enter the plains of India.

g) *Kosi*: The Kosi river system drains eastern Nepal. It is also known as the Sapt Kosi as seven major rivers form this river system. These are--
- the Sun Kosi river which rises beyond the Gosainthan massif
- the Indrawati river which drains the eastern outer rim of the Kathmandu valley
- the Bhola Kosi river which drains the snow-melt waters of the Cho Oyu and Gauri Shankar massifs
- the Dudh Kosi which drains the Mount Everest massif, the highest group of peaks in the world
- the river Arun which rises in the trans-Himalayan zone of Tibet. It has cut a fantastic gorge across the main Himalayan range near the Everest massif
- the Barun river rises from the Barun glacier at the base of the Makalu. It flows into the river Arun

— the river Tamur which is the eastern tributary of the river Kosi. It rises from the snows on the western flank of the Kanchanjunga group of peaks known as the Kumbhakaran Himal.

Brahmaputra River System

The Brahmaputra river system drains the eastern Himalaya. It ranks amongst the longest rivers of the world. It rises in Tibet where it is known as the Tsang Po and flows in an easterly direction in southern Tibet before making a U-turn and entering India as the Dihang or Brahmaputra.

This river is joined by a number of tributaries emanating both from the eastern Himalaya and from other north-eastern states. The main eastern Himalayan tributaries of the Brahmaputra are—
— the Teesta river rises from the Zemu glacier on the eastern slopes of the Kanchanjunga massif. Its tributaries include the Lhonak, Lachung and Rangit rivers
— the Torsa river enters Bhutan as the Amo Chu from the Chumbi valley
— the Raidak river system drains a part of western Bhutan. Its tributaries are the Thi Chu and Paro Chu
— the Manas river system drains a part of Bhutan and Arunachal Pradesh. Its tributaries include the Mangde Chu, Chamke, Kurd and Tawang rivers
— the Kameng river rises from the Kangto group of peaks. Its tributaries are the Bichom and Tenga
— the Subansiri river is another major tributary of the Brahmaputra river.

Glaciers

Glaciers too form a part of the drainage of the Himalaya. Negi (1982) states, "A glacier is a naturally moving body of large dimensions made up of crystalline ice (*neve* in the upper layers) formed on the earth's surface as a result of accumulation of snow".

A large number of glaciers occur in the Himalaya. A majority of these are found on the main Himalayan range and the ranges lying to the south of it, viz the Karakoram and Zaskar ranges. Others occur on the offshoot ranges such as the Dhauladhar and Pir Panjal. The altitude to which Himalayan glaciers may descend varies with the following conditions—

-- aspect and slope
-- total annual precipitation in the form of snow
-- latitude.

Himalayan glaciers descend to lower elevations in Kashmir than the ones in the eastern Himalaya. This has clearly been brought out in the following table--

Glacier	Region	Lowest elevation (in mts.)
Chandanwari	Kashmir	3200
Gangotri	Garhwal	4000
Khumbu	Nepal	4200
Zemu	Sikkim	4300
Lunana	Bhutan	4450

The effect of aspect on glaciation in a particular mountain slope is mainly due to differences in the solar radiation received by them. South-facing slopes have a relatively less ice cover. In the same way areas receiving more annual precipitation in the form of snow are heavily glaciated.

It has been estimated that an area of about 32,000 sq kms is under a permanent cover of ice and snow in the Himalaya. This amounts to about 17 per cent of the total geographical area of the Himalaya. Higher concentration of glaciers in the Himalaya lie in the tracts having the highest mountain peaks viz, Nanga Parbat, Nun Kun, Kinner Kailash, Bandarpunch, Chaukhamba, Nanda Devi, Nanda Kot, Dhaulagiri, Annapurna, Everest, Makalu, Kanchanjunga and Chomolhari.

Important glaciers of different parts of the Himalaya are listed below--

Jammu and Kashmir--Siachen, Hispar, Baltoro and Biafo.

Himachal Pradesh--Chandra, Bhaga, Chandra-Nahan and Beas Kund.

Garhwal and Kumaun--Yamunotri, Gangotri, Satopanth, Milam and Pindari.

Nepal--Api, Annapurna and Khumbu.

Sikkim--Zemu and Kanchanjunga.

Bhutan--Chomolhari, Masang Kang and Lunana.

Arunachal Pradesh--Bichom and Kangto.

Recession

An outstanding feature of Himalayan glaciers is that many of them are shrinking or retreating. However, on the other hand recent data collected from the few Himalayan glaciers which are kept under annual observation suggest that there has been a considerable slowing down in the recession of these glaciers. Bhandari and Nijanpurkar (as cited by Negi 1990) state, "Several Himalayan glaciers have been studied using this technique (viz mass balance studies), for example the Nehnar in Kashmir, the Gora in Himachal Pradesh and the Changme Khangpu in Sikkim. The studies found that most glaciers had a negative mass balance during the past decade, that is more ice is melting than the snow is accumulating. That glaciers have been receding is also evident because several tributaries once connected with the main body of the glaciers are now disconnected--a consequence of the severe negative mass balance. If this trend continues, the consequences could be severe."

Glacial erosion becomes a problem in the areas vacated by receding glaciers. Ritcher (1898) writes, "The material loosened by weathering is removed by the glacier or slides off over the *neve* to form either actual moraines or at least *neve* moraines. These walls do not bury themselves in their own debris and in consequence continually offer fresh surfaces for attack. Finally, the weaning away of the cirque floor by the glacier cooperates to keep the cirque walls on a steep angle and facilitates avalanching."

Major Glaciations in the Himalaya

Major cycles of glaciation are known to have occurred in the Himalaya in the past. Four glacial and corresponding inter-glacial periods were initially identified from the Karewa sediments of Kashmir, thus establishing a parallel with Europe. However there is confirmed evidence of the later three glaciation periods in the Himalaya. The evidences include--

-- Old glacial morainic ridges formed either along the flanks of the glaciers or deposited at the lower end of the glacier
-- U-shaped valleys in the middle hills
-- Epigenetic gorges.

The existence of very old and extensive periods of glaciation has at times been confirmed by the wide and straight stretches along the course of some river valleys in the Himalaya. However, this evidence is not always conclusive.

Glaciers as a Source of Water

Himalayan glaciers are important ever-renewing sources of freshwater for the millions living in the plains of northern and eastern India. In summer and autumn, large quantities of water melts from the glaciers and flows down the rivers and streams draining the Himalaya. Fresh snow is added to the glaciers in winter. Thus the permanent reservoir of ice in the Himalaya is very large. It has been estimated that a single glacier of the size of the Gangotri glacier has a total volume of over 20 cubic kilometres of ice as against the total maximum reservoir capability created by a very large dam like the Bhakra of less than 8 cubic kilometres (Vohra 1981).

Glaciers and Floods

Glaciers are often the cause of floods. The peak melting season of glaciers coincides with the arrival of the monsoons. It overlaps the monsoon season in the eastern Himalaya. In river basins where the monsoons are weak, the melt-water acts as a substitute for precipitation. However, in basins where there is ample rainfall from the monsoons, the melt-water adds to the flow of the rivers and streams and causes floods.

In many glaciated areas, as the sun rises, the level of the melt-water in the streams rises. This causes flash floods at mid day. This is a common phenomenon in many glaciers. Cases of unwary travellers and cattle being washed away in such flash floods have come to light.

Moraines block the flow of the melt-water and form morainal lakes. With the passage of time, this debris dam gives way, causing the water to drain away with considerable force, thus resulting in flash floods.

Lakes

Hundreds of lakes of varying sizes occur in different parts of the Himalaya. On the basis of their origin, Himalayan lakes may be classified into the following:

a) *Salt lakes*: These are estuarine lakes in Ladakh. They do not have an outlet and serve as inland drainage basins for rivers and streams that flow into it from the surrounding areas, e.g., Tso Morari lake. The water of these lakes is salty and deposits of salt are found along their banks.

b) *Glacial lakes*: These lakes have been formed in and around glaciers in depressions formed by the glacier, e.g., Chandra Tal lake.

c) *Remnant lakes*: These are the remnants of vast lakes that covered the entire valleys, e.g., Dal lake.

d) *Natural dam lakes*: These lakes are temporary in nature. They are formed when a natural dam (usually a landslide) blocks the flow of a river or stream. However it drains away once the debris dam bursts, e.g., Gohana Tal lake in Garhwal which drained away and caused flash floods in the Alaknanda valley in 1970.

e) *Structural lakes*: These lakes are formed by folds or faults due to movements in the earth's crust, e.g., Nainital lake.

Himalayan Rivers

AGLAR RIVER

This is a major Himalayan tributary of the river Yamuna. It rises as a number of small streams fed by underground water on the western slopes of the ridge separating the drainage of the Yamuna and Bhagirathi to the west of Tehri. Thereafter the Aglar runs along an east-west direction to join the Yamuna river near a place called Yamuna bridge. The small streams draining the northern slopes of the Mussoorie ridge contribute their water to this river.

Thatur is the most important village lying along the course of this river. The massive Nag Tibba ridge lies on the northern flank of this river and contributes waters to it.

ALAKNANDA RIVER

This is the most important river draining the central part of U.P. Himalaya. This river rises as a small gurgling stream in the glaciers to the north of the temple town of Badrinath. In its initial stages this river runs in a SW direction and washes past the feet of the holy Lord Badri Vishal temple. A number of small snow-fed streams join this river near Badrinath.

Thereafter it makes into a deep gorge near Hanuman Chatti, downstream of which it begins to flow in a more or less SSE direction. Enroute this river is joined by a number of tributaries—

-- the river Vishnuganga joins it at Vishnuparyag. This small hamlet is also the starting point for the journey to the famous Valley of Flowers
-- the river Nandakini joins it at Nandparyag
-- the river Pindar joins it at Karnparyag. This small town lies on the road to Gwaldam and further on to Kumaun
-- the river Mandakini joins it at Rudraparyag. This town lies at the gateway to the famous Kedarnath valley.

The river Alaknanda finally merges with the Bhagirathi river at the temple town of Deoparyag to form the river Ganga.

In its downhill journey, the Alaknanda river has formed a number of broad open valleys. It is believed that these were once lakes formed as the Alaknanda was temporarily blocked during various phases of the uplift of the Himalaya. The vast terraces at Gauchar and Srinagar bear testimony to this contention. The town of Srinagar is today one of the largest towns in Garhwal.

This river has carved out deep V-shaped valleys, incised meanders, gorges, terraces and broad valleys in its journey to meet the Bhagirathi at Deoparyag. A number of landslides occur in the valley of this river. These are at Pipalkoti, Nandparyag and Kaliasaur near Srinagar.

In July 1970, a tragedy occurred in the Alaknanda valley. A natural debris dam had blocked a tributary of this river at Gohana tal. After a fortnight of incessant rains this dam burst and caused widespread destruction in the entire Alaknanda valley.

A number of hydel projects have come up along this river.

AMO CHHU RIVER

Another name of the Torsa river that drains western Bhutan. (For detailed description, see 'Torsa river').

AMRIT GANGA RIVER

The Amrit Ganga river is a tributary of the Dhauliganga river in Garhwal. It rises from the Bankund glacier which lies in a huge amphitheatre encircled by a horse-shoe-shaped jagged ridge having a number of cirques and horns. Five snow-fed channels join the Amrit Ganga river in the valley of the Bankund river. These are--

-- two channels flow down from the slopes of the peaks of Rataban and Nilgiri in the south
-- three channels flow down from the slopes of the Deoban peak in the west.

Besides these tributary channels, many hanging glaciers on the slopes of the Kagbhusand peak facing north drain their waters into the main valley of the Bankund glacier from which flows the Amrit Ganga river.

Extensive deposits of ground moraines are overlain by steps of terminal moraines and ridges of lateral moraines in the upper catchment of this river. The Amrit Ganga flows along a remarkable braided pattern once it comes out of the valley of the Bankund glacier. River terraces have formed along its lower course. It flows into the Dhauliganga river near Gamsali.

Dry alpine and sub-alpine vegetation is found in the Amrit Ganga catchment. The alpine meadows are visited by graziers in summer. There are small human settlements along this river.

ANDHI KHOLA RIVER

The Andhi Khola river is a glacier-fed tributary of the Gandak river. It originates from the snowy wastes on the slopes of the Annapurna massif, flows towards south, then from east to west for a short distance before cutting a gorge across the lower Himalaya or Mahabharat Lekh and merging with the Gandak or Krishna Gandaki river.

A permanent blanket of snow covers the upper catchment of this river. Hanging valleys bearing small glaciers open into the main glacial trough. Fluvio-glacial sediments are strewn all over the valley bottom.

The water descends along a very steep gradient over waterfalls and rapids. It flows between huge boulders and unsorted sediments. The valley is narrow with steeply sloping sides. Terraces occur at various levels on both flanks of the valley.

Alpine meadows and scrub is found on the valley bottom and in depressions in the upper catchment. Fir, spruce, birch and blue pine forests occur at lower elevations together with deciduous forests. The Andhi Khola valley is sparsely populated.

ANDRA RIVER

The Andra river is a tributary of the Pabar river which in turn drains into the Tons river. This river rises from a small glacier tenanted in a cirque of the lower hills of the main Himalaya in the area to the north-west of Chargaon in Shimla district of Himachal Pradesh. Thereafter it flows in a general direction towards south-east and merges with the Pabar river at Chargaon.

Precipitous slopes encircle the upper catchment of this river from all sides. Small glaciers located in hanging valleys on either flanks of the Andra valley pour their discharge into the mainstream.

A deep valley has been carved by this river. River-cut and river-built terraces occur on either sides of the valley. Other prominent geomorphic features of this tract include spurs, ridges, rock benches and steep cliffs.

The Andra multipurpose hydro-electric project has been constructed by utilising the waters of this river. A dam has been erected across the Andra river about 10 kms upstream of Chargaon. It provides water to the power house at Chargaon.

Fir and spruce forests occur at higher elevations. These give way to chir pine and oak forests in the valley. Small human settlements have come up along the river Andra.

ARU RIVER

The Aru river is a major tributary of the Liddar river in the Pahalgam area of Kashmir. The Aru glacier located in a cirque of the main Himalayan range on the periphery of the Kashmir valley is the source of this river. Small channels from the snowy wastes of the Aru glacier merge to form the Aru river. The snout of this glacier is littered with morainic deposits. Thereafter the Aru river flows in a general direction towards south-east and joins the Liddar river at the mountain resort of Pahalgam.

The upper valley of this river is U-shaped. It has been carved by the action of glaciers. There occur moraines all along the river bed. The water descends over a series of rapids and small waterfalls before entering a V-shaped valley with interlocking spurs. Small river terraces have been formed at various levels along the middle and lower course of the Aru river.

Alpine meadows occur on the moraines in the upper valley. These are visited by graziers in summer. Sub-alpine and temperate coniferous and deciduous forests are found at lower elevations in the Aru catchment. Small villages have come up along the middle and lower course of this river.

ARUN RIVER

The Arun river is one of the three major tributaries of the Kosi river system that drains eastern Nepal. It drains the central part of the Kosi catchment. This is a trans-Himalayan river rising from the snowy wastes of southern Tibet. Thereafter it flows in a general direction towards south. It crosses the Nepal-Tibet border along a deep gorge and continues to flow southwards. The Arun river flows into the mainstream of the Kosi river a short distance upstream of the Chatra gorge.

A number of tributaries join the Arun river at various places. These are--

-- two small streams rising from a glacier on the north-facing slope of the Everest massif join the Arun river in southern Tibet near the Nepal-Tibet border
-- a tributary from the western flank of the Arun river joins the mainstream in its middle course.

This river flows along a V-shaped valley with incised meanders and rock benches. The near vertical walls of the upper valley descend right upto the river bed. Other geomorphic features include river terraces, spurs, cliffs, ridges and hanging valleys.

Alpine, sub-alpine and temperate vegetation is found in the Arun catchment. The higher reaches are under a permanent cover of snow. A number of large villages have come up along this river.

ASAN RAO RIVER

The Asan Rao river is a large Siwalik tributary of the Yamuna river in the Dehradun valley of Garhwal. It rises from the base of the Mussoorie ridge and flows in a general direction towards south-west to flow into the Yamuna river near Herbettpur.

Two small spring-fed streams emanating from the limestone caves at the base of the Mussoorie ridge merge to form the Asan Rao river. It flows across the western part of Dehradun valley to its mouth.

The terrain in the upper catchment of this river is very steep. The river enters the Dehradun valley in its upper course and the gradient becomes gentler. Thereafter it meanders across the valley bottom. It is joined by a number of spring-fed tributaries. These include the Song (Asan Rao), Chor Khala and Sansaru Khala streams.

Broad river terraces have developed along the middle and lower courses of this river. They are under cultivation. Sub-tropical forests occur in the upper catchment of the Asan Rao river. Many settlements have come up along this river. This includes Anarwala and Dakrani.

ASHNI RIVER

The Ashni river is a tributary of the Giri river which in turn drains into the river Yamuna. It rises as a small spring in the area to the north-east of Shimla. Thereafter this river flows in a general direction towards south-east to join the Giri river near Sadhupul in the Chail area.

This river flows along a deep V-shaped valley whose side slopes vary from steep to precipitous. It has carved a steep gorge across the offshoots of the Nag Tibba ridge. It then makes a sharp turn and enters a wider valley.

The main geomorphic features of the catchment of the Ashni river are interlocking spurs, incised meanders, paired and unpaired terraces, cliffs and small channel islands and rock benches. River terraces occur high up the valley slopes. This is indicative of the level at which the Ashni river once flowed. Numerous small spring-fed tributaries join the Ashni river at various places along its course.

Sub-tropical chir pine, oak, khair and shisham forests are found in the Ashni catchment. These are severely degraded due to heavy biotic pressure.

ASTOR RIVER

This is a tributary of the Indus river. It rises in a glacier on the north-facing slopes of the Great Himalayan range near Burzil pass in the Ladakh tract of Jammu and Kashmir. Thereafter it flows in a NW direction and joins the river Indus soon after it emerges from the main Himalayan gorge a little downstream of Bunji. This river drains the area lying to the east of Nanga Parbat.

Many small snow-fed streams originating from different depressions on the Great Himalayan range join the river Astor in its short course. Its catchment is made up of U-shaped valleys, glacial moraines, eskers, cirques and steep slopes. It is largely devoid of a vegetative cover.

AWA RIVER

This river rises from the Dhauladhar range in the Kangra valley of Himachal Pradesh. It flows in a south-westerly direction before joining the river Beas. The river Awa receives water both from snow-fed as well as rain-fed smaller tributaries. The catchment consists of steep slopes and broad terraces that have been formed by the river over the past millions of years.

BABAI RIVER

This is a short Siwalik river of the foothills of western Nepal. The Babai river originates on the south-facing slopes of the lower Himalaya in the area to the west of Bijauri. Thereafter it flows in a dun valley between the lower Himalaya in the north and the Siwalik hills in the south and has cut a narrow gorge across the Siwaliks before entering the plains of India where the Babai joins the Ghagra river.

The Babai emanates as a spring from the reservoir of underground water. It has a very steep gradient in its upper course which becomes gentle once the river enters the dun valley. Here it is joined by small tribrutries flowing in both from the lower Himalaya in the north and the Siwalik hills in the south.

This river enters a narrow gorge across the Siwalik hills. Boulders are strewn all over the river bed. The Babai is in spate during the monsoon season as the degraded hills are unable to absorb the rainwater that pours down in a short span of time.

Sub-tropical sal and pine forests are found in the Babai catchment. Bijauri and Kumbher are two important towns of this tract though they are not situated along the river bed.

BAGADARI GAD RIVER

The Bagadari gad river is a small tributary of the Dudhganga river in Garhwal. It is fed by a valley glacier.

BAGMATI RIVER

The Bagmati river drains the famous Kathmandu valley of Nepal. It rises from the snows to the north of the valley and winds its way across the flat Kathmandu valley. Thereafter it flows towards southeast, then south-west to enter the plains of north Bihar where it merges with the Ganga river system.

Geologists are of the opinion that this river was blocked by a natural dam near Chhobar as a result of the upliftment of the Himalayan mountains. This produced a vast lake in what is now the Kathmandu valley. After sometime this natural dam burst and the lake drained away thus exposing the lake bottom which now bustles with human life.

Downstream of the Kathmandu valley the Bagmati river flows past interlocking spurs and a V-shaped valley towards the plains. It flows through a dun valley before cutting across the Siwalik hills on the Indo-Nepal border to enter the plains. Wide terraces have been formed along this river in the foothills.

Thick temperate and sub-tropical forests occur in the catchment of this river both within and outside the Kathmandu valley. These are subjected to heavy biotic pressure. The Kathmandu valley is densely populated and is the largest town in Nepal. Others include Patan, Bhaktapur and Pashupatinath.

BAIRA RIVER

This is a small snow-fed river that rises from the snows on southern slopes of the Pir Panjal range in Himachal Pradesh. It flows in a south-easterly direction before joining the river Siul, which is a tributary of the Ravi river. The course of the Baira river lies entirely between the Pir Panjal range in the north and the Dhauladhar in the south.

Its catchment consists of steep slopes, deep valleys and terraces that have been slowly laid down by the river. Numerous small tributaries join the Baira river before it finally merges with the Siul river. These are fed by the snows on the southern face of the Pir Panjal range.

BALKHILA RIVER

The Balkhila river is a tributary of the Alaknanda river. It drains the famous Mandal valley of Garhwal. This river rises from the Lal Mati glacier and flows in a general direction towards south-east to merge with the Alaknanda river near Chamoli.

This river is in the form of a small stream in its upper reaches. Ancient glaciers have carved its valley. There occur extensive moraines and fluvo-glacial deposits all along the Balkhila river from its origin to its confluence with the Alaknanda.

The Chandra Shila stream is a major tributary of this river. It joins the Balkhila river in the uplands. A number of other snow-fed streams join the main river at various places all along its course.

Alpine and sub-alpine forests are found in the upper catchment of the Balkhila river. These are replaced by temperate vegetation in the lower reaches. Dense forests also occur along the various tributary streams of the Balkhila river. A number of small human settlements have come up along the Balkhila river.

BANER RIVER

This river is also known as the Baner khad. It is a tributary of the Beas river and drains the central part of the Kangra valley. The Baner river rises as a small snow-fed channel on the southern slopes of the Dhauladhar range near Palampur. It is joined by another stream flowing in from the west at a distance of about 1 km from its origin. The Baner river then flows for another 2 kms before meeting a large tributary draining the north-western slopes of its catchment. Another stream flowing in from the north-east joins the Baner river a short distance upstream of its confluence with the Beas river.

The general direction of flow of the Baner river is towards southwest. Huge boulders cover the river bed in its upper course. The water seems to wind its way past these boulders. The river bed widens as it reaches the valley bottom and the gradient becomes gentler.

Large terraces occur on either side of this river in its middle and lower courses. These are under cultivation. Temperate and sub-temperate forests are found on the upper slopes. Many human settlements have come up along the river Baner.

BANGANGA RIVER

This is a tributary of the river Beas. It joins the main river in the Kangra valley of Himachal Pradesh. The Banganga river rises from the southern slopes of the Dhauladhar range. Its catchment is comprised of steep slopes, V-shaped in its upper reaches and broad open valley near its confluence with the river Beas. Large fertile sediments have been formed all along the river near its mouth.

The river Banganga is fed by snow-melt waters and channels emanating from springs. A number of small settlements have sprung up all along the course of this river.

BANKUND RIVER

It is a tributary of the Amrit Ganga river in Garhwal. It rises from the Bankund glacier.

BARMA GAD RIVER

The Barma Gad river is a major tributary of the Dudhganga river which in turn is a part of the Alaknanda river system of Garhwal. It rises from the snout of a small glacier located in a trough west of the Kalapani glacial trough which feeds the Dudhganga river.

The glacial trough from which this river rises has a number of small hanging valleys on either sides. These contain perpetual deposits of ice which feed streams that flow into the main channel of the Barma Gad river.

Immediately downstream of the glacial trough there occurs the famous Barma alpine meadow along this river. It is a vast expanse of deposits laid down by glaciers in the past. A carpet of grass covers the Barma meadow which blooms with flowers in late autumn.

The Barma meadow extends to the Rudranath meadow, downstream along this river. Many small channels of water flow across these meadows and merge with the Barma Gad river.

The Barma Gad river in turn flows into the Dudhganga river about 4 kms to the east of Rudranath temple. This Barma Gad valley is visited by migratory grazier communities during the summer season. They move down to the sheltered valleys in winter.

BARODA GAD RIVER

The Baroda Gad is a major tributary of the Bhilangana river which in turn drains into the Bhagirathi river at Tehri. This river originates from the Shastru tal group of glacial lakes located in the cirque of the Shastru peak in the northern part of Tehri district. The Shastru tal is a group of glacial lakes. These lakes feed the river Baroda Gad.

This river flows along a U-shaped valley in its upper tract. A number of small hanging valleys open into the main valley at various places. These too drain snow-melt waters. In its lower course this river has carved a V-shaped valley which is lined on both banks by a series of river formed terraces. This flows into the Bhilangana in its upper course near the mountain hamlet of Ghamsali.

The upper catchment of this river is devoid of a vegetative cover. Alpine, sub-alpine, temperate and sub-tropical forests are found at different elevations in the Baroda Gad catchment. Small human settlements have come up at various places along the middle and lower courses of this river.

BARUN RIVER

This is an important river of the Kosi river system that drains eastern Nepal. It rises as small channels from a glacier on the south-facing slopes of the main Himalayan range in north-eastern Nepal near the border with Tibet. Thereafter it flows in a general direction towards south and contributes its waters to the Kosi river system.

The Barun river flows along a V-shaped valley except in its upper reaches where the valley has been carved by the action of glaciers. The river has formed terraces at various levels. Alpine, sub-alpine and temperate vegetation is found in this tract. A number of villages exist along the Barun river.

BASPA RIVER

This is an important tributary of the river Satluj in its upper courses. The river Baspa rises in the snowy wastes of the extreme north-eastern corner of Himachal Pradesh. A number of snow-fed water channels combine to form the main river. Thereafter it flows along a NNW direction past a steep gorge that is clothed on either sides by a good vegetative cover. Enroute it is joined by many smaller channels draining snow-melt waters.

The Baspa river has cut a gorge across the main Himalayan range. Thereafter it empties itself into the river Satluj. Numerous small settlements have come up along the course of this river.

Steep slopes and U-shaped valleys occur in the upper catchment of this river. Further downstream it has cut a spectacular gorge. River terraces are found at many places in the Baspa valley.

BATA RIVER

The river Bata originates in the boulders below the Nahan ridge in the south-western corner of Himachal Pradesh as the Jalmusa-ka-khala. It is mainly fed by rainwater that is cycled as underground water before finally coming up on the surface as a spring. Thereafter it flows along a SSE direction across the Paonta valley before emptying itself into the Yamuna river downstream of Paonta town.

This river flows below the surface for a part of its length in its upper reaches. The river bed is dry and covered by a thick pile of sediments in this tract. Thereafter the water flows on the surface. The waters from the Giri river are led through a tunnel to the power house at Girinagar after which they are led into the Bata river. This has immensely increased the discharge of this river.

Sal, khair and sissoo forests are found on either banks of this river. Large open terraces have been formed by it. These are both paired and unpaired. A number of small tributary streams which join this river in the Paonta valley are--

-- Khara-ka-khala flowing in a southerly direction from the Nahan ridge
-- Kanser khala originating from the southern slopes of the Nahan (Kanser) ridge.

BEAS RIVER

The river Beas is a major tributary of the Indus river. It drains the central and south-central part of Himachal Pradesh. This river rises at the foot of a small glacier lying on the southern slopes of the massive Pir Panjal range near the famous Rohtang pass at an elevation of about 4000 metres. It drains past the famous holiday resort of Manali and through the Kulu valley south of which it has cut across the Dhauladhar range at Larji.

The gradient from the Rohtang massif to Larji is very steep. The river has formed a broad open valley downstream of Kulu. It is believed that this valley too was once a lake that was formed when the Beas river was temporarily blocked by upheavals in the Himalayan mountain chain. Later on the lake waters drained away and the present day valley came into being. Large terraces occur on either sides of the river in Kulu valley.

The main tributaries of the river Beas before it cuts across the Dhauladhar range are--
- a number of small tributaries rising from near Beas kund on the Rohtang massif join the main river
- the river Parbati flows into the Beas river near the town of Shamshi
- the Patlikhul river joins the Beas river
- the Harla river joins the Beas river near Bhuntar
- the river Tirthan flows into the Beas river near the mountain hamlet of Larji
- the Sainj river too joins the Beas near Larji.

Downstream of Larji, the river emerges out of the Dhauladhar range as a milder torrent for the gradient is gentler than that in its upper reaches. Thereafter it drains past the bustling town of Mandi and takes a westerly course across the southern part of Kangra valley. The Pandoh dam has been erected across the Beas river upstream of Mandi. It has formed a vast artificial lake.

The important tributaries which rise from the Dhauladhar range and join the Beas in the Kangra valley are--
- the rivers Uhl, Suketi, Luni, Awa, Banganga, Gaj and Chaki.
- Large terraces occur along the river as it flows across the Kangra valley.

The river Beas enters the plains of Punjab near Pathankot after cutting across the Siwalik range.

BHADAL RIVER

The river Bhadal is one of the two snow-fed channels that join to form the Ravi river. It rises from the snowy wastes on the western slopes of a N-S trending ridge lying between the Pir Panjal and Dhauladhar ranges in the Bara Banghal area of cental Himachal Pradesh. It flows in a westerly direction before merging with the Tant

Gari river to form the mainstream of the Ravi.

The river has a steep gradient. Its catchment is made up of U-shaped valleys, waterfalls, moraines, cirques and towering peaks. It is joined by numerous small snow-fed water channels.

Narrow paired and unpaired terraces have developed on both the banks of this river. These are strewn with angular and sub-angular rocks that have been brought down by the river and glaciers in the past. Its lower catchment is densely vegetated while the upper reaches are devoid of a vegetative cover. A number of small human settlements occur along this river.

BHAGA RIVER

This river originates from the snowy wastes of southern slopes of the main Himalayan range in the Lahul area of Himachal Pradesh. A number of small snow-fed water channels join to form this river. Thereafter it flows in a SSW direction as a raging torrent before joining the river Chandra near Keylong to form the Chenab river.

U-shaped valleys, waterfalls, glaciers and moraines characterise the upper catchment of the Bhaga river. Its gradient is very steep in this tract. Thereafter it reaches the valley bottom. The valley is open and lined by river terraces on either banks. The entire tract is devoid of a vegetative cover. Trees occur only along the river bed and channels of snow-fed streams that empty themselves into this river at different places.

The discharge of this river increases during the summer months when the snow on the high mountains surrounding this tract melts. Very heavy snowfall is received during the winter months and this river freezes for short periods from time to time.

BHAGIRATHI RIVER

The river Bhagirathi is one of the two most important rivers which merge to join the Ganga at Deoparyag. It rises from near Gaumukh at the snout of the Gangotri glacier lying at the base of the Chaukhamba peak in Uttarkashi district of Garhwal. Thereafter it flows in a southerly direction in the initial stages before turning towards SW and then its course is towards SE near the confluence with the river Alaknanda. The upper catchment of the Bhagirathi river is glaciated. Numerous glaciers and ice fields give rise to small channels which in turn empty themselves into the main river.

This river has cut spectacular gorges in its middle course where it has cut through granites and crystalline rocks of the central Himalayan axis. Small terraces cling to the slopes bearing testimony to the fact that the river once flowed at higher levels.

A V-shaped valley has been formed in the lower course of this river. Its speed is greatly reduced in this tract. Broad paired and unpaired terraces occur on either banks of the river.

In its rush to meet the Alaknanda at Deoparyag the Bhagirathi river flows past many towns and smaller settlements. These are Gangotri, Uttarkashi and Tehri. The main tributary of this river is Bhilangana which joins the Bhagirathi river at Tehri.

A gigantic dam is being constructed across the Bhagirathi river at Tehri known as the Tehri dam which will submerge the existing township of Tehri. This dam will provide power and irrigation water to millions of people living both in the surrounding hills and plains.

BHAKRA (U.P.) RIVER

The Bhakra river is a small Siwalik river of the U.P. hills. It is fed by a number of small springs that rise from the south-facing slopes of the lower Himalaya. Thereafter this river flows through gorges across the low rolling Siwalik hills before entering the Ganga plains.

The catchment of this river is under various stages of degradation due to the high biotic pressure on its sub-tropical and riverine forests. Its discharge goes up drastically in the rainy season but drops down to a small trickle during the hot summer months.

A number of human settlements have come up along the Bhakra river. The large river terraces are under cultivation.

BHANDAL RIVER

The Bhandal river is a large rain-fed tributary of the Song river in the Dehradun valley of Garhwal. It rises as a spring emanating from the reservoir of underground water at the base of the Mussoorie ridge that is made up of a thick deposit of limestone. Thereafter this river rapidly descends down the foothills to enter the valley bottom. A number of springs containing sulphur join the Bhandal river at a place known as Sahastradhara. It is a famous picnic spot. The water is known for its curative properties.

The gradient changes once the Bhandal river enters the valley bottom. Its floor is strewn with boulders of various sizes that have been brought down by the river in the past thousands of years. The Bhandal river flows into the mainstream of the Song river upstream of

Lachhiwala.

Sub-tropical deciduous forests occur in the upper catchment of this river. Riverine vegetation is found along its middle and lower courses. There also occur large tracts of cultivated land and patches of sal forests along the lower course of this river. A number of human settlements exist along the Bhandal river. These include Sahastradhara and Raipur.

Limestone quarrying has degraded the upper catchment of this river. Huge debris have brought down mining waste right upto the river bed.

BHERI RIVER

The Bheri river is a large tributary of the Ghagra river system draining western Nepal. The mainstream of this river rises from the north-facing slopes of the Dhaulagiri massif in north-central Nepal. It flows towards west along a U-shaped valley, turns towards south-west where it has cut a deep gorge across the lower Himalaya or Mahabharat Lekh, then flows parallel to the Siwalik hills for a short distance in its lower course before merging with the Ghagra.

A large number of snow-fed tributaries join the Bheri river at various places. These are--

-- a northern tributary rising from the area east of Phijargaon joins the Bheri in its glacial trough
-- another tributary rises to the east of Charkabhotgaon, flows to the south of it, takes right angle turn and joins the Bheri river in its upper course
-- an east-west flowing tributary rises near Dharpatan and flows into the Bheri near Jajarkot.

The upper catchment of this river has been carved by the action of glaciers. It has cut a deep gorge across the lower Himalaya near Salyan. River terraces of various sizes have been formed along this river.

Rich alpine, sub-alpine and temperate forests are found in the upper and middle valleys of the Bheri river. Sub-tropical forests in various stages of degradation occur in the lower valley. Salyan is the largest town in the Bheri catchment.

BHILANGANA RIVER

This is the most important tributary of the river Bhagirathi. It rises from the Khatling glacier north of Ghuttu in Tehri district of

Garhwal. The river flows along a SW direction to join the Bhagirathi river at Tehri in the Bhagirathi valley. A number of glacial lakes occur in the upper catchment of this river. Small streams emanate from these waterbodies and merge with the mainstream. The topography of the upper catchment of the Bhilangana river consists of U-shaped valleys, moraines, eskers, cirques and high ridges. Permanent pockets of snow occur in the moist, shady depressions. In its upper course, the Bhilangana flows past alpine meadows and thickets of sub-alpine forests.

The middle course of this river is relatively gentler. Terraces lie along both the banks. Many small rivulets and streams join the Bhilangana river at this stage. Coniferous and broad-leaved forests are found in the Bhilangana valley. The gradient evens out in the lower course before its confluence with the Bhagirathi.

The river Bhilangana flows past a number of small hamlets and settlements. These include Ghuttu in the upper reaches and Ghamsali.

BHOGA RIVER

The river Bhoga drains the lower hills in the south-western corner of Jammu and Kashmir. It rises as a small spring in the Siwaliks to the west of Jammu. Groundwater and rainwater account for the discharge of this river. Many small tributary streams coming from different directions join it. This river flows in a SE direction before merging with the river Chenab.

The upper catchment of the river Bhoga consists of steep slopes, rills, gullies and landslides. The forests are highly degraded due to a heavy biotic pressure in the form of lopping and grazing. Unconsolidated sediments occur naturally in the Siwalik hills and this has added to the unusual levels of soil erosion that is taking place in this tract.

Large terraces are found along the middle and lower courses of the river Bhoga. These are under various forms of cultivation. A number of human settlements have come up along the river in this tract.

Flash floods usually occur in the river Bhoga and its tributaries during the monsoon season. The degraded hills are unable to absorb the vast quantity of water that pours down from the skies during a short span of time. Thus it flows on the surface and causes flash floods. The river Bhoga is gradually engulfing a large tract of land along its bed each year.

BHOLA KOSI RIVER

This is an important tributary of the Kosi or Sapt Kosi river system. It drains the snow-melt waters of the Cho Oyu and Gauri Shankar massifs. The snow-melt waters of the Cho Oyu glacier forms the Bhola Kosi river. The upper catchment of this river has been carved by the action of glaciers.

BHYUNDAR RIVER

The river Bhyundar river is an important tributary of the Alaknanda river. It is formed by the river Pushpawati that rises from the east Kamet glacier. The Pushpawati river combines with a tributary from the east to give rise to the Bhyundar river near the mountain hamlet of Ghangharia on the trail to Hemkund and the Valley of Flowers.

Thereafter the Bhyundar river flows in a SE direction to merge with the Alaknanda or Vishnuganga flowing in from the NW at Vishnuparyag. The Bhyundar is a fast flowing river draining a densely vegetated catchment. Alpine meadows occur in its upper catchment which give way to sub-alpine, temperate coniferous and deciduous forests in the middle and lower reaches. The terrain has been carved by glaciers at high elevations and by the action of running water near its confluence with the Alaknanda.

BICHOM RIVER

This is an important tributary of the Tenga river system which drains a part of Arunachal Pradesh. It rises as a small channel on the south-facing slopes and flows along a steep gradient to join the main river. A number of smaller channels join the Bichom river.

The upper catchment of this river consists of very steep slopes, V-shaped valleys and incised meanders. Terraces occur on both sides of the river in its middle and lower courses. Dense forests are found in the entire catchment of this river. A number of human settlements of various sizes also occur along the Bichom river.

BINDAL RIVER

The river Bindal flows through the town of Dehradun in Garhwal. It is fed by a number of springs at the base of the towering Mussoorie ridge to the north of Dehradun. Underground water feeds this river all round the year though its discharge becomes very low during the hot summer months.

Steep slopes of the Mussoorie ridge form the upper catchment of this river. Thereafter it enters the longitudinal valley of Dehradun and flows along a gentle gradient. Large river terraces occur on either sides of the river all along its course through the Dehradun valley. In fact the old town is situated on two paired terraces of the river Bindal.

It flows through the town in the form of a trickle. Human settlements have come up even on the river bed. However there is a significant increase in its discharge during the monsoon season. In certain patches the river is eroding its banks.

Good sal forests are found in the upper course of the river near the hamlet of Rajpur, while khair and shisham forests occur along the lower course of this river. Dehradun town has developed in its middle course.

BRAHMAPUTRA RIVER SYSTEM

The Brahmaputra river system drains the eastern Himalaya. It is one of the longest rivers in the world. The total length of this river from the source to the sea is 2900 kms. This river rises in the great glacier of the Kailash range just south of the lake Konggul Tsho in southern Tibet. Thereafter this river flows in an easterly direction in a deep gorge through a remote and inaccessible area of southern Tibet. It has a length of about 1609 kms in Tibet and is known as the Tsang Po.

After this, the river Brahmaputra takes a great loop at the base of the Namche Barwa peak and enters Indian territory as the Brahmaputra. It flows through the Assam valley for a considerable distance before debouching into the Bay of Bengal through a series of distributaries.

Thus, the drainage basin of this system drains almost the entire eastern Himalaya. It extends from the south-eastern slopes of the Kanchanjunga massif on the border of Nepal and Sikkim to the eastern extremity of the Himalaya. The entire northern tracts of this vast drainage basin is made up of towering snow-clad peaks of the main Himalayan mountain wall. The general slope of the Brahmaputra basin is towards south.

Middle and lower Himalayan hills account for the central part of this basin. These are densely forested. Low rolling foothills occur in the southern tract. Very heavy rainfall is received in the entire Brahmaputra basin from early June to early September. Winters are very cold and snowfall occurs in the higher reaches.

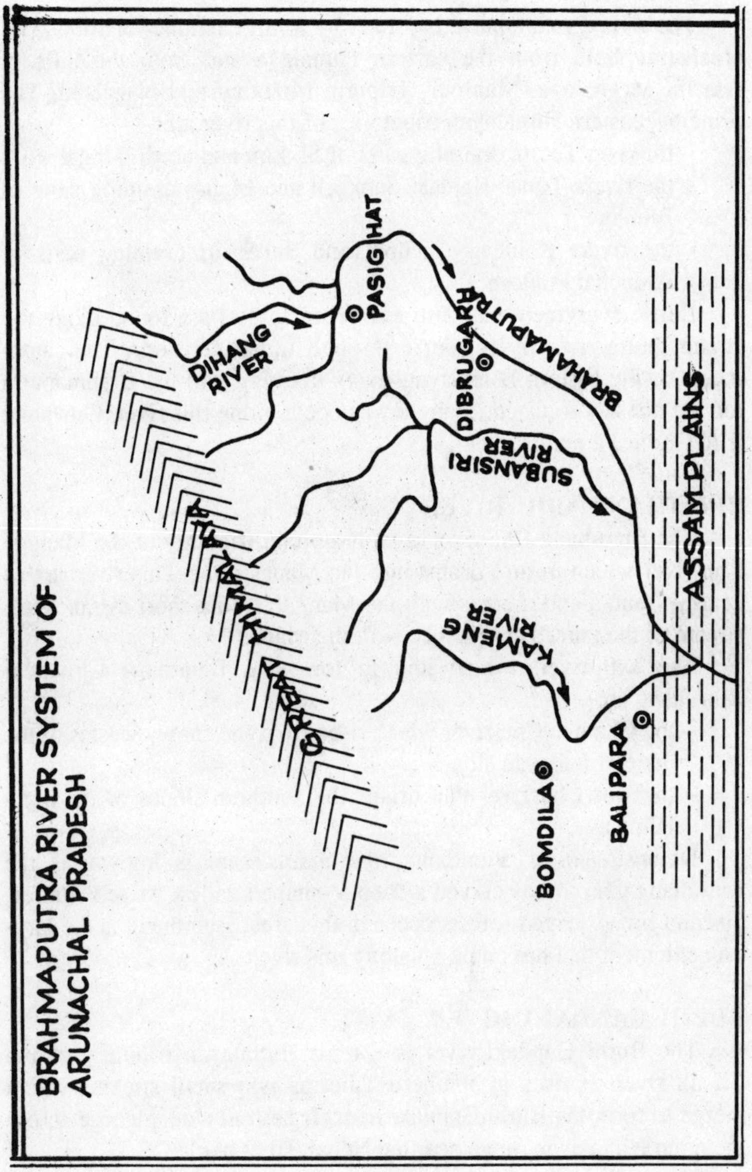
BRAHMAPUTRA RIVER SYSTEM OF
ARUNACHAL PRADESH
DIHANG
RIVER
PASIGHAT
DIBRUGARH
BRAHAMAPUTRA
SUBANSIRI
RIVER
KAMENG
RIVER
ASSAM PLAINS
BOMDILA
BALIPARA

The river Brahmaputra is joined by a large number of tributaries emanating both from the eastern Himalaya and from the hills of Assam, Meghalaya, Manipur, Tripura, Mizoram and Nagaland. The principal eastern Himalayan tributaries of this river are--
-- the river Teesta draining parts of Sikkim and north Bengal
-- the rivers Torsa, Raidak, Sankosh and Manas draining parts of Bhutan
-- the rivers Kameng, Bichom and Subansiri draining parts of Arunchal Pradesh.

Dense evergreen and semi-evergreen forests are found along the Brahmaputra river in its course through Indian territory. The catchments of the eastern Himalayan rivers draining into the Brahmaputra too are densely forested. Many towns occur along this river. Guwahati is the largest amongst them.

BUMTHANG CHU RIVER

The Bumthang Chu river is an important tributary of the Mangde Chu river which in turn drains into the Manas river. This river drains central Bhutan and merges with the Mangde Chu a short distance upstream of the latter's confluence with the Manas.

The two rivers which join to form the Bumthang Chu near Bumthang are--
-- the Chamke Chu river which rises from the snowy wastes of the main Himalayan slopes
-- the Dur Chu river that drains the southern slopes of the main Himalaya.

Downstream of Bumthang, the mainstream is known as the Bumthang Chu. It has carved a deep V-shaped valley. Mixed coniferous and broad-leaved forests occur in this area. Bumthang is the largest settlement that has come up along this river.

BURHI GANDAKI RIVER

The Burhi Gandaki river is a trans-Himalayan tributary of the Trisuli river. It rises in southern Tibet as two small streams which merge to form the Burhi Gandaki river. It has cut a deep gorge across the main Himalayan range near the Nepal-Tibet border.

Thereafter this river flows in a general direction towards south to merge with the Trisuli river downstream of Nuwakot. A small tributary flowing in from the north-east merges with the Burhi Gandaki river a short distance upstream of its mouth.

The valley of this river is narrow. The water flows amongst huge boulders. Terraces occur on both flanks of its valley. Alpine, sub-alpine and temperate forests are found along the lower and middle courses of this river while the upper tracts are under a permanent cover of snow.

CHAKI RIVER

The river Chaki is an important river draining the south-western part of Himachal Pradesh. It rises as small snow-fed and rain-fed streams from the southern slopes of the Dhauladhar range. Thereafter it flows in a more or less south-easterly direction through western Kangra. This river enters Punjab near Pathankot and joins the Beas river.

Steep to very steep slopes occur in the upper catchment of the Chaki river. Snow remains in the moist shady depressions of the Dhauladhar range all through the year. It feeds the headwaters of this river. The terrain becomes gentler as the river enters the valley bottom in its middle course. It has deposited an enormous quantity of sediments of various sizes in the form of terraces in this tract. These are under cultivation. Numerous tributaries rising from the Dhauladhar range merge with the river Chaki in the Kangra valley.

Its slows down considerably in its lower course near the H.P.-Punjab border and enters Punjab as a huge slow-moving channel of water. Many settlements lie along the Chaki river. Nurpur is the most important amongst these.

CHAMKE CHU RIVER

The Chamke Chu river is a tributary of the Bumthang Chu river that drains central Bhutan. Two small glaciers lying in the south facing slopes of the main Himalaya feed this river. Their melt-water channels merge to form the Chamke Chu river. It flows in a general direction towards south south-east before merging with the Dur Chu river to form the Bumthang Chu.

The Tang Chu is the most important tributary of the Chamke Chu river. It flows into the latter a short distance upstream of the Chamke Chu-Dur Chu confluence.

A part of the Chamke Chu catchment is under a permanent cover of snow. The moraines are covered with alpine meadows while temperate forests are found at lower elevations.

CHANDRA RIVER

The river Chandra is one of the two rivers which merge to form the Chenab in Lahul area of Himachal Pradesh. It rises in the snows lying at the base of the main Himalayan range in Lahul and Spiti district. Thereafter it flows for a considerable distance along the base of this range in a SE direction before making a 180° turn and taking a SW course in Spiti valley. It flows on to merge with the Bhaga river downstream of Keylong.

The upper and middle catchments of this river are made up of a topography that has been carved out by glacial action. The entire area is a vast cold desert that receives little or no rain as it lies in the rain shadow of the Pir Panjal range lying towards south. Many small snow-fed tributaries join the Chandra at different places.

Describing its course Harcourt (1871) states, "The river Chandra passes through a totally barren land where there are no signs of life, the solemn mountains clad in eternal snow lying on its either flanks. No villages adorn its banks, no attempts at cultivation, no human life are met with and nothing greets the eye but the never ending monotonous cliffs, which are lopped by the fierce stream as its rushes in wild fury against its banks . . . ."

Koksar is the only important human settlement that lies along this river.

CHANDRA-BHAGA RIVER

In its upper course through Lahul valley, the river Chenab is known as the Chandra-Bhaga. It is formed by the rivers Chandra and Bhaga and hence the name. As it flows through Lahul, this river has laid thick deposits of sediments. It is in spate during the summer season when the snow on the mountains melts. Flash floods occur with regularity in the early afternoon in summer. They have been known to wash away hundreds of cattle each year. The river Chandra-Bhaga may freeze occasionally during the winter season. (For detailed description of Chandra-Bhaga see 'Chenab river').

CHANDRAPURI GAD RIVER

This is a small tributary of the Mandakini river in Garhwal. It flows into the mainstream at the mountain hamlet of Chandrapuri in Chamoli district.

CHANG CELMO RIVER

The Chang Celmo river is a tributary of the Shyok river which joins the Indus river in Ladakh. This river originates from a large glacier on the western slopes of the Lanak La pass on the eastern border of Ladakh and Tibet. The Chang Celmo river then flows towards west along the northern base of an offshoot range of the Karakoram before flowing into the Shyok river a short distance downstream of Shukpa Kuzang.

Snow-covered high mountains encircle the Chang Celmo valley from all sides. The water-divide between Ladakh and Tibet is in the east. There is a small gap in its northern flank near Pamzal village, where a large tributary flowing in from a glacier in the north-west joins the mainstream. The river descends along a series of rapids. A thick deposit of sediments has been laid down along the river bed. The Chang Celmo river may freeze during the winter season. It is in spate in late summer when the snow in its catchment melts at a fast pace.

The Chang Celmo valley is bleak and remote. Vegetation is sparse. Pamzal is one of the few human settlements that have come up along this river. The trail from Chushul to Lanak La crosses this valley.

CHAPURSAIN RIVER

This river drains the extreme north-western part of India. It rises in the glaciers on the northern slopes of the Karakoram range and flows in an easterly direction before merging with the river Khunjerab to form the river Hunza.

A number of glacial melt-waters merge to form the Chapursain river. They descend over hanging valleys and moraines to give birth to this river. The entire catchment of this river has been carved out by glacial action. The important topographic features include U-shaped valleys, moraines, glacial depressions, eskers, cirques, amphitheatres and steep razor sharp ridges.

The river Chapursain descends over a very steep gradient in its upper and middle courses. Its speed is slower near its confluence with the river Khunjerab. The entire catchment is devoid of vegetative cover. There is virtually no human settlement in the valley of the river Chapursain. The river is in spate in late summer when the snow in the high mountains melts at a very fast pace and releases a huge volume of water into this river.

CHAUKA RIVER

Another name of the Ghagra river as it flows through a longitudinal dun valley in the foothills of western Nepal. (For detailed description see 'Ghagra river').

CHAVAL CHHU RIVER

The river Chaval Chhu is a tributary of the Subansiri river system which drains a large part of Arunachal Pradesh. It rises in the snows on the southern slopes of the main Himalayan range. The gradient in the upper course of this river is very steep. The river flows along a deep V-shaped valley and past terraces and incised meanders.

The middle course of the Chaval Chhu river too is made up of steep slopes and gorges. Thereafter it merges with the Subansiri river system. The entire catchment of this river is covered with dense forests. Small human settlements have come up along its middle and lower courses.

The river Chaval Chhu is in spate during the monsoon season when a vast quantity of water is received in its catchment from the SW monsoons. It flows through the narrow channel and causes the river to overflow its banks.

CHENAB RIVER

This is an important tributary of the river Indus which flows through the Himalaya. It rises as the rivers Chandra and Bhaga in Lahul and Spiti district of Himachal Pradesh. Thereafter it is known as the Chandra-Bhaga. The river Chenab flows in a north-westerly direction through the cold desert valley of Lahul. In its middle course it enters the famous Pangi valley which bears thick virgin forests. Many small snow-fed nalas and rivers join the river Chenab in its upper and middle courses. Prominent amongst these are--

-- the Miyar nala that joins the Chenab in Lahul
-- the Saichu nala that merges with the Chenab in Pangi valley.

It flows along the northern base of the Pir Panjal range before entering the Doda area of Jammu and Kashmir and it has cut across this range through a spectacular gorge. Thereafter it flows along the southern base of this range before flowing southwards and entering the plains. The important Himalayan tributaries of the Chenab which join it in its lower course are--

-- the river Jammu Tawi
-- the river Bhoga

CHENAB RIVER SYSTEM IN H.P.

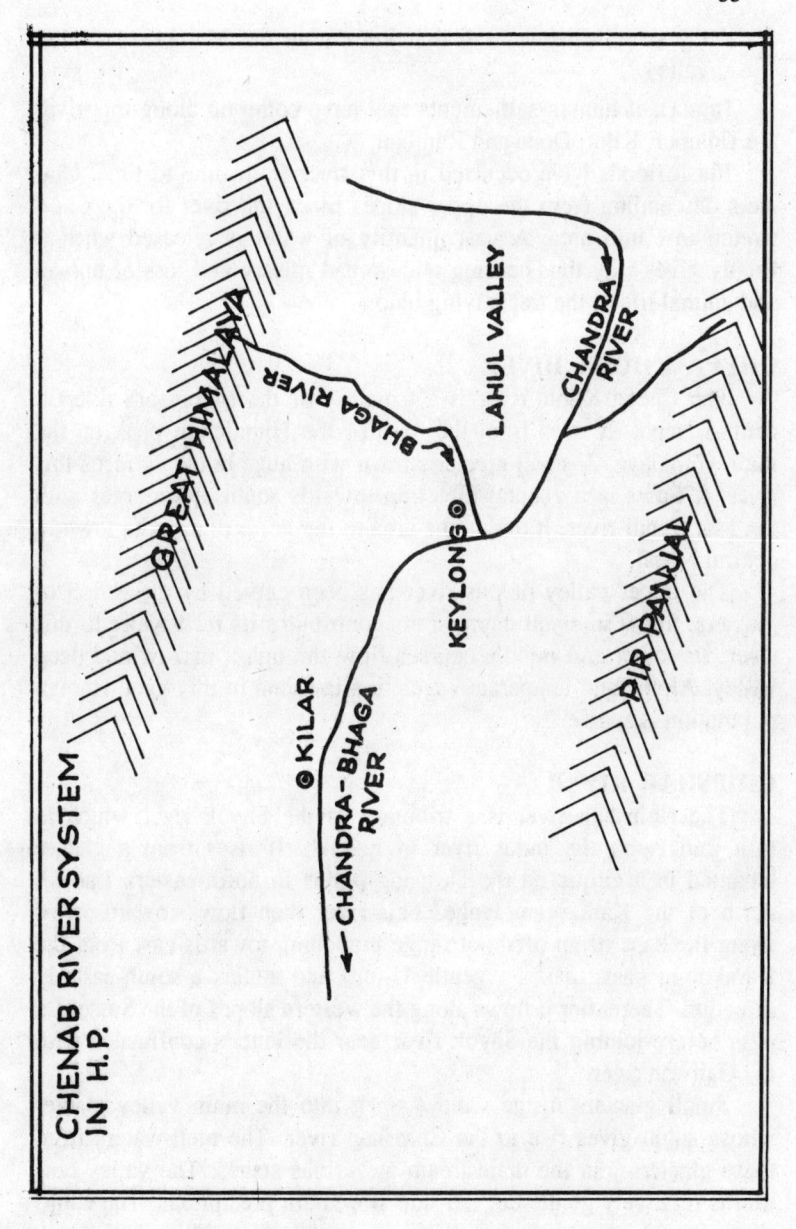

- GREAT HIMALAYA
- BHAGA RIVER
- LAHUL VALLEY
- CHANDRA RIVER
- KEYLONG
- KILAR
- CHANDRA-BHAGA RIVER
- PIR PANJAL

-- the river Munawarwali that joins it in the Munawarwali dun valley.

Important human settlements that have come up along this river are Udaipur, Kilar, Doda and Ramban.

Flash floods have occurred in this river from time to time. Glaciers descending from the upper slopes block the river for days at a stretch in Pangi area. A vast quantity of water is released when it finally gives way thus causing widespread misery and loss of human and animal life in the tracts lying below.

CHEPA KHOLA RIVER

The Chepa Khola river is a tributary of the Marsyandi river in central Nepal. It rises from the base of the Himalchuli peak on the main Himalaya. A small glacier strewn with huge boulders feeds this river. It flows in a general direction towards south and merges with the Marsyandi river. It drains the area to the north of Gorkha town in central Nepal.

The upper valley of this river has been carved by the action of glaciers. Snow in small depressions contributes its melt-water to this river. Its lower and middle courses flow through a narrow and deep valley. Alpine and temperate vegetation is found in this tract. Human population is sparse.

CHIPSHAP RIVER

The Chipshap river is a tributary of the Shyok river which in turn joins with the Indus river in Ladakh. It rises from a glacier tenanted in a cirque on the Despang plains in north-eastern Ladakh north of the Karakoram range. This river then flows towards west along the base of an offshoot range branching towards east from the Karakoram pass, makes a gentle U-turn and attains a south-easterly direction. Thereafter it flows along the western slopes of the Sasser La pass before joining the Shyok river near the latter's confluence with the Galiwan river.

Small glaciers inside valleys open into the main valley glacier whose snout gives rise to the Chipshap river. The melt-waters from these glaciers join the mainstream at various stages. The valley bottom is relatively gentle but the side slopes are precipitous. The Chipshap river descends over a series of rapids and small waterfalls. A major snow-fed tributary flows into the main river just as it begins to take a U-turn. The western slopes of the Sasser La pass are very steep and extend right upto the river bed. Moraines are strewn all over the valley floor.

Virtually no vegetation exists in the catchment of the Chipshap river. The trail from Sasser La to the Karakoram pass crosses the Chipshap valley.

CHOUBAG GAD RIVER

This is a snow-fed tributary of the Girthi river in Garhwal. It flows into the mainstream in its lower course.

CHUS RIVER

This is a small snow-fed tributary of the Shyok river in Ladakh. It flows in from south-east from the Chushul area.

DABKA RIVER

The Dabka river is a small spring-fed channel of the Siwalik or outer Himalaya of Uttar Pradesh hills. It rises from the reservoir of underground water on the slopes of the low-rolling Siwalik hills. Thereafter it flows in a general direction towards south and enters the Ganga plains.

The entire catchment of this river is degraded. The forests are under an intense biotic pressure and hence a vast quantity of sediment is flowing down the river Dabka. Sub-tropical forests occur in the catchment of this river. Flash floods are a common occurrence during the monsoon season.

DARONDIA KHOLA RIVER

This is a tributary of the Marsyandi river in central Nepal. It rises from the snowy wastes on the southern slopes of the main Himalaya. This river flows towards south-east in its upper course and then changes direction to flow in a south-westerly course to join the Marsyandi river which in turn is a part of the Gandak catchment.

Alpine, sub-alpine and temperate forests are found in this tract. The upper reaches are under a permanent cover of snow. Gorkha is a large town along the Darondia Khola river.

DHANSIRI RIVER

The Dhansiri is a river of the south-eastern part of Bhutan. It rises as a spring in the lower Himalaya in the area to the south-east of

Tashigang. The Dhansiri river flows in towards south-east in its upper course, turns west and then attains a south-easterly direction once again. This river enters the plains after cutting a gorge across the outer foothills in the extreme south-eastern corner of Bhutan.

The Dhansiri catchment is relatively smaller in extent as it rises in the lower Himalaya. A number of tributaries join this river at various places. The valley is V-shaped while the side slopes vary from very steep to precipitous. The river bed is strewn with unsorted sediments ranging from large boulders to sandy gravels.

Alpine, sub-alpine, temperate and semi-evergreen forests are found in the Dhansiri catchment. A part of its catchment is under cultivation. Human settlements have come up along the Dhansiri river.

DHAOLI GANGA (KALI) RIVER

The Dhaoli Ganga river is a tributary of the Kali river in Pithoragarh district of Kumaun. It rises as two snow-fed mainstreams from valley glaciers on the southern slopes of the Kumaun-Tibet waterdivide. These two channels join after emerging from their U-shaped valleys. Thereafter the Dhaoli Ganga river flows in a general direction towards south-east to merge with the Kali river flowing in from the north near Dharchula.

The upper catchment of this river has been carved by the action of glaciers. It is a rain-deficient tract. Small hanging valleys containing side glaciers open into the main valley at various places. The snow-melt waters from these glaciers join the Dhaoli Ganga river at various points in its upper and middle courses. Spring-fed streams empty themselves into the river in its lower course.

The Dhaoli Ganga river flows along a deep V-shaped valley in its middle and lower courses. There occur small river terraces along this river. These are under cultivation. Alpine and sub-alpine forests are found in the upper catchment of this river. Temperate and sub-tropical forests are found at lower elevations. A number of small human settlements have come up along the middle and lower courses of this river.

DHAULIGANGA RIVER

The Dhauliganga river is a tributary of the Alaknanda river system of Garhwal. It rises from a glacier on the southern slopes of the Niti pass located on the border of Garhwal and Tibet. It collects waters from the numerous small channels flowing down from the glaciers to the east. The Ganesh Parbat has formed an amphitheatre in the west. Many hanging glaciers feed channels that flow into the Dhauliganga river near the Ganeshganga camping ground.

Thereafter this river descends along a gentle gradient for about 2 kms to the Geldhung camping ground which is situated on a glacial moraine. Thereafter the river flows along a broad U-shaped valley carved by glaciers. It becomes narrow towards its mouth.

Many snow-fed tributaries drain into the Dhauliganga river at various places. These include—
- the Parla river collects water from the Parla cirque. It drains small channels from hanging glaciers. This river drains into the Dhauliganga at the Geldhung camping ground
- the Kamet river is fed by these glaciers. It merges with the Dhauliganga river near Geldhung
- the Janti Gad river rises from Kalajabra-Chorhoti peak. It joins the Dhauliganga near Ghamsali
- the Amritganga river rises from the Bankund glacier and drains into the Dhauliganga near Ghamsali
- the Girthi river rises from near Kungribingri peak and flows in from the east to join the Dhauliganga river near Kailashpur.

Avalanches commonly occur in the upper catchment of this river. The village of Timmersen was destroyed by one such avalanche a few decades back.

Dry temperate and alpine vegetation occurs in the catchment of this river. Amongst the human settlements that have come up in this tract are Geldhung, Niti and Kailashpur.

DHAWALGANGA

This is another name given to the Bhyundar river. (For a detailed description see 'Bhyundar river').

DIHANG RIVER

Another name for the Brahmaputra river as it flows through eastern Arunachal Pradesh. This river enters Arunachal Pradesh from Tibet as the Tsang Po through a gorge acorss the main Himalaya upstream of Jido. Thereafter it descends rapidly past interlocking spurs formed by the lower and outer Himalaya to enter the plains near Sadiya as the Brahmaputra.

A large tributary rising from the main Himalaya near Tunga pass and draining the Abor hills joins the Dihang river near Kebang. Another small river flows into the mainstream from the right flank of the catchment at a short distance downstream of Kebang.

The entire tract through which this river flows in Arunachal Pradesh is densely forested. The small settlements that have come up along this river in Arunachal Pradesh are Jido, Bomdo, Riga, Kebang and Pasighat. (For detailed description see 'Brahmaputra river').

DIKRANG RIVER

The Dikrang is a small river of the lower hills of south-central Arunachal Pradesh. It rises as two channels on the south-east-facing slopes of the Silung (Abor) hills. These channels get water from springs. They merge to form the mainstream of the Dikrang river after about 20 kms. Thereafter this river flows in a general direction towards east before making a loop and flowing in a south-westerly direction and turning towards south-east as it enters the Brahmaputra plains. The Dikrang river flows into the Brahmaputra river near Bordutighat.

This river flows along a relatively open valley in the lower hills. Broad river terraces occur along the river. It meanders across the foothills in its lower course. The entire catchment of this river bears rich evergreen, semi-evergreen and sub-tropical forests.

The Dikrang river is in spate during the monsoon season. Sagali, Noju, Sikhi, Lipi and Nadar are the small towns that exist along this river.

DIURI RIVER

The Diuri river is a short tributary of the Manas river in eastern Bhutan. It rises from the middle hills of east-central Bhutan and flows in a general direction towards south to merge with the Manas river.

This river flows past a series of incised meanders or interlocking spurs. The river bed is strewn with boulders of various sizes. Many tributaries emanating from springs join the Diuri river at various places. The catchment of this river is degraded due to high intensity of landslides and accelerated erosion.

Temperate and sub-temperate conifer and broad-leaved forests occur in the catchment of this river. A considerable part of the total land area is under cultivation. Small villages have come up along the Diuri river.

DRAS RIVER

The river Dras is an important tributary of the river Shigar (south) which in turn drains into the Indus at Marol. This river rises from the snowy wastes and small glaciers on the northern face of the main Himalayan range. Thereafter this river flows towards north to merge with the Shigar (south) river.

Small rivers fed by glacial melt-waters combine to form the Dras river. The terrain resembles a typical glaciated topography. It consists of amphitheatres, hanging valleys, morainal deposits, eskers and cirques. In its lower reaches the river slows down to a considerable extent. Terraces of various sizes occur all along the course of the Dras river.

The entire catchment is devoid of a vegetative cover as it lies in the rain shadow of the main Himalayan range. Scanty vegetative growth has come up in a narrow strip along channels formed by snow melt waters. The discharge of the river Dras rises drastically in late summer when it receives a large quantity of water from the melting snow.

DUDHGANGA RIVER

The Dudhganga river is a part of the Alaknanda system. It rises from the snout of the Kalapani glacier which is located in the cirque of the Vishnudhar ridge. Hence this river is also known as the Kalapani Gad river. The glacier has a length of about 5 kms and its trough is upto a kilometre wide. There are no hanging valleys in the trough of this glacier.

This river rapidly flows down a deep gorge which starts from the bottom of this U-shaped trough. It is fed by a number of tributaries draining snow-melt waters. These include--
   -- the river Barma Gad rising from a glacial trough to the east of the Dudhganga trough. It flows into the mainstream near the famous Rudranath temple
   -- the rivers Gaira Gad, Bagadari Gad and Rikhi Gad flow into the Dudhganga river at various places.

The higher elevations of the Dudhganga catchment do not bear a vegetative cover as they lie above the snowline. Alpine meadows are found in depressions and on the thick deposits of moraines that occur in the upper catchment of this river. Sub-alpine birch and rhododendron forests, temperate coniferous and deciduous forests are found in the middle and lower catchments of the Dudhganga river. Human habitation is in the form of a few villages along the middle and lower courses of this river. Shepherds move upto the alpine meadows in summer.

DUDH KOSI RIVER

The Dudh Kosi river is a tributary of the Sun Kosi river which in turn is a part of the Kosi river system draining eastern Nepal. The mainstream of this river rises from the glaciers and snow fields on the southern slopes of the Everest massif.

Thereafter the Dudh Kosi river flows over an almost endless series of rapids in a general direction towards south to merge with the Sun Kosi south of Okhal Dhunga. As the water rushes over the cascades it presents a milky look and hence the name.

This river flows along a deep gorge. There is a vertical drop of over 150 metres in the side walls of the Dudh Kosi river. Small river terraces are found at different levels. The upper catchment of this river is in the form of a huge glacial amphitheatre. A tributary draining the eastern part of the Dudh Kosi river joins the mainstream near Okhal Dhunga.

Snow covers the upper tracts of its catchment. Alpine meadows and scrub are found along the river in its upper course. Sub-alpine and temperate coniferous and deciduous forests are found in the middle and lower catchments of this river. A number of large villages have come up in this tract. These include Namche bazar and Okhal Dhunga.

DUR CHU RIVER

This is a small tributary of the Bumthang Chu river in Bhutan. It rises from the snows on the southern slopes of the main Himalayan range.

GAIRA GAD RIVER

This is a small snow-fed tributary of the Dudhganga river in Garhwal.

GAJ RIVER

Also known as the Gaj Khad, this is an important tributary of the river Beas. It rises as small streams from the snows on the southern slopes of the Dhauladhar range in Kangra area of Himachal Pradesh.

These streams combine to form the river Gaj.

Steep slopes occur in the upper catchment of this river. These have been carved out by the action of both running water and glaciers. A razor-sharp ridge forms the northern limit of this boundary. A sparse vegetative growth covers the upper slopes.

The gradient levels out once the river reaches the valley in its middle and lower courses. Paired terraces of various sizes occur on either banks of the river. These are under cultivation. The river has exposed a dry bed with the water channel meandering across it. Numerous tributary streams join the river Gaj at various places. Most of them originate from the southern slopes of the Dhauladhar range.

The Gaj river joins the Beas a little upstream of the Pong dam lake.

GAJ KHAD

Another name of the Gaj river. (For detailed description see 'Gaj river').

GALIWAN RIVER

The Galiwan river is an important tributary of the Chipshap river which in turn drains into the Shyok river in the north-eastern part of Ladakh in Jammu and Kashmir. The mainstream of this river rises near the Depsang plain at an elevation of over 5000 metres. The points of origin of the rivers Galiwan and Chipshap are near each other.

This river then follows a south-westerly course before joining the Chipshap. Another channel of the Galiwan river comes in from the east. It is fed by a number of snow-fed streams originating from glaciers lying above. They form a tributary channel before merging with the Galiwan river a little upstream of the latter's confluence with the Chipshap.

The entire catchment of this river is glaciated. Tongues of ice descend down from the mountains. It is completely devoid of a vegetative cover. There is no human habitation in this tract and it is very desolate and remote. Waters from the snow that melt very rapidly in summer cause the water level to rise very fast in the early afternoon every day during this season.

GANDAK RIVER

The Gandak system drains central Nepal. The main river of the

Gandak system is the Kali Gandaki or Krishna Gandaki. It rises in the trans-Himalayan tract of Manang Bhot in north central Nepal near the international border with China. Thereafter this river flows in a general direction towards south. The upper catchment of this river system is bleak and desolate. It lies in the rain-shadow of the main Himalayan range. Vegetative growth is very poor and is restricted to strips along the mainstreams or channels formed by snow-melt waters that drain into it. Small glaciers are the source of water to the mainstream and its tributaries. The terrain has been carved by the action of glaciers.

The river has cut a spectacular gorge across the main or great Himalayan range that lies to the south of its source between the Dhaulagiri and Annapurna massifs. This gorge has a drop of hundreds of feet.

The middle and lower courses of this river system in Nepal flow through V-shaped valleys, incised meanders and have paired and unpaired terraces on either sides. Forests of different types and composition cover the catchment. The other important rivers of Gandak system are--

-- the river Seti Gandak which rises from the base of the Annapurna Himal massif. It drains the famous Pokhra valley before joining the mainstream
-- the river Marsyandi flows north of the Annapurna Himal massif and turns south in the tract between it and the Manaslu
-- the river Trisuli rises from the Ganesh Himal and joins the Gandak system.

The combined Gandak has cut across the lower hills of south central Nepal. It flows through the densely forested Chitwan valley to enter the plains of India. It finally empties itself into the Ganga river.

GANESH GANGA RIVER

This is a small tributary of the Dhauliganga river in Garhwal. It is fed by a glacier on the southern slopes of the main Himalayan range.

GANGA RIVER

The river Ganga is formed at the confluence of the rivers Bhagirathi and Alaknanda at Deoparyag. However strictly speaking, the river Ganga rises as the Bhagirathi from the snowy wastes of the Gangotri glacier in Uttarkashi district of Garhwal. (For detailed description of the Bhagirathi see 'Bhagirathi river').

Downstream of Deoparyag the Ganga river flows through a deep,

V-shaped valley. It has cut across the lower Himalayan range near Saknidhar through a fantastic gorge. Very small river terraces occur occasionally along this river in its journey to the plains from Deoparyag. Poor lower Himalayan deciduous forests are found in this tract.

The Ganga valley opens up near Rishikesh where the river emerges from the lower Himalaya into the dun valley. Thereafter it flows over a gently sloping terrain. This river has cut across the Siwalik hills lying in the south at Hardwar to enter the plains of northern India. The main towns and other human settlements which lie along this river from Deoparyag to the plains are Lakshman Jhula, Muni-ki-Reti, Rishikesh, Virbhadra and Hardwar.

GANGA RIVER SYSTEM

The drainage basin of the Ganga river system covers about one third of the western Himalaya and the entire central Himalaya. This basin extends from the eastern face of the Shimla ridge in Himachal Pradesh to the south-western slopes of the Kanchanjunga massif on the Nepal-Sikkim border; thereby including parts of Kinnaur, Shimla, Solan and Sirmur districts of Himachal Pradesh, Garhwal, Kumaun and Nepal.

High towering peaks of the main Himalayan mountain wall form the northern boundary of the Ganga basin. The general slope of the land is towards south. There occur large glaciers tenanted on the main slopes of the main Himalaya. The peaks soar to elevations of over 6000 metres.

Middle and lower Himalayan ranges occupy the central part of this basin. The low rolling Siwalik hills occur in the south. The climatic conditions vary from sub-tropical in the lower hills to arctic in areas above the snowline. Very heavy rainfall is received from late June to mid-September. Snowfall occurs in the upper tracts all through the severe winter months from mid-November to March. A thick blanket of snow covers the ground for several weeks at a stretch during this season. Summers are mild except in the lower hills where the maximum temperature may soar to about 40°C.

The main tributary systems of the Ganga system are--
-- the river Yamuna and its tributaries
-- the rivers Bhagirathi and Alaknanda
-- the Kali river and its tributaries draining eastern Kumaun and western Nepal
-- the Ghagra river system draining western Nepal

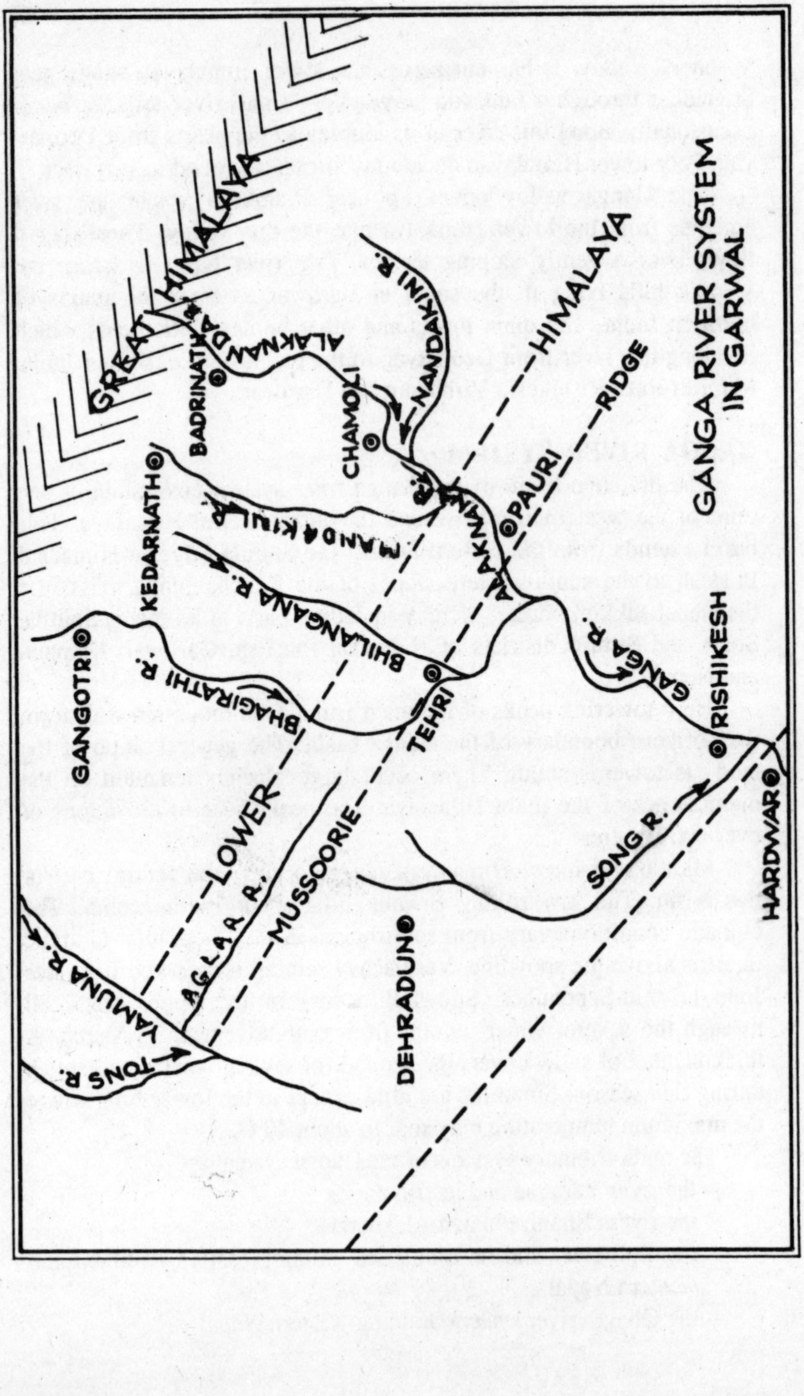

GANGA RIVER SYSTEM IN GARWAL

-- the Gandak river system draining central Nepal
-- the Kosi river system draining eastern Nepal.

Other smaller tributaries which drain directly into the Ganga include the Song and Ramganga.

GEMRI RIVER

The Gemri river is a tributary of the Manas river in eastern Bhutan. This river originates as a small channel from a boulder-strewn glacier located on the south-facing slopes of the main Himalayan range. It is joined by numerous snow-melt water channels flowing in from different directions.

The glacial trough from which the Gemri river originates has a gently sloping bottom while the side slopes are precipitous. Glacial sediments occur along the river bed. The water flows over a series of small waterfalls and rapids.

The valley becomes narrow downstream of the glacial trough. The gradient is steep and the river has cut a deep gorge across the lower Himalaya. Terraces occur on both sides of its valley.

Alpine grasslands and scrub are found on the moraines in the glacial trough. Mixed conifer and broad-leaved forests are found at lower elevations. A part of lower catchment of this river is under cultivation.

GHAGRA RIVER

The river Ghagra and its tributaries drain western Nepal. It rises from the snowy wastes on the southern slopes of the main Himalayan range near the border with Tibet. Thereafter it flows in a general direction towards south through a deep, V-shaped valley. This river pierces the lower Siwalik hills near Gaindakanda to enter the plains of India.

The upper catchment of this river has been carved by glacial action while that of the middle and lower courses has been influenced by the action of running water. The entire tract is under a vegetative cover whose condition varies from area to area.

The river Ghagra is joined by a number of important rivers. These are--

-- the river Karnali is the largest river draining into the Ghagra. It rises in Tibet and flows for a considerable distance in western Nepal before merging with Ghagra. The river Seti is an important tributary of the Karnali

-- the river Bheri rises in the snows of the Dhaulagiri massif. Its waters enter the mainstream of the Ghagra river in the lower hills of Nepal.

GHENGAR KHALA RIVER

This is a small spring-fed tributary of the Lastar Gad in Tehri district of Garhwal.

GHIZAR RIVER

The river Ghizar is an important tributary of the Gilgit river. It rises as a small-snow melt channel from the glaciers on the northern slopes of the great or main Himalayan range in the north-western corners of Jammu and Kashmir. Thereafter it flows towards east to join the Gilgit river flowing in from the north.

The entire catchment of the Ghizar river is bleak and desolate. The slopes are devoid of a vegetative cover. The topography has been sculptured by the action of glaciers. Prominent geomorphic features include U-shaped valleys, glacial amphitheatres, lakes, moraines and waterfalls.

Many small tributaries join the river Ghizar at various places along its course. These rise from the glaciers on either sides of the Ghizar valley. The river descends along a steep gradient in its upper and middle courses, while its speed is reduced near the confluence with the Gilgit river and the valley becomes wider. It is strewn with boulders of varying shapes and sizes that has been brought down by the river from the high mountains. Virtually no human settlements occur along this river.

GHUJERAB RIVER

The river Ghujerab rises from the snows to the north of the Karakoram range in the extreme north-north-western part of Jammu and Kashmir. It is an important tributary of the Hunza river which in turn joins the Gilgit. The Ghujerab is a very short river. It is fed by two main streams, one flowing in from the SE while the other from the NW. Both these feeder streams are fed by glaciers that descend down from the high mountains.

Downstream of the confluence of the two feeder streams, the Ghujerab river flows towards west to merge with the mainstream of the Hunza river coming in from the north-east. This river flows along a very steep gradient. Small terraces formed by deposits brought down by running water occur on either banks of the river.

The entire catchment of this river is devoid of a vegetative cover. The slopes are very steep and the topography has been carved by the action of glaciers. No human habitation occurs in this tract.

GILGIT RIVER

The Gilgit river is an important tributary of the Indus river in Ladakh area of Jammu and Kashmir. It originates from a glacier near the extreme north-western boundary of the Himalaya. Thereafter it has cut across an offshoot of the Karakoram range and flows in a southerly direction before it is joined by the Ghizar river flowing in from the west. The Gilgit river then flows eastwards and merges with the Indus at Bunji just before the latter river has cut a path through the main Himalayan range.

The entire catchment of the Gilgrit river is bleak and desolate. Vegetative growth is extremely poor and consists of low forms of plant life occurring along water channels from spring to autumn each year. Bunji is the main human settlement along this river.

Important tributaries of the Gilgit river are--

--the river Ghizar is the major right bank tributary of the Gilgit river. It joins the main river in its middle course

--the river Hunza is the major left bank tributary of the Gilgit river. It originates from beyond the Karakoram range and merges with the mainstream in its lower course a little upstream of Bunji.

GIRI RIVER

The river Giri is an important tributary of the Yamuna. It drains a part of south-eastern Himachal Pradesh. This river rises as a small spring fed by underground waters to the NNE of Shimla. Thereafter it flows in a south-westerly course for a considerable distance before taking a south-easterly alignment. In its upper course the Giri river has formed a deep, V-shaped gorge across the Nag Tibba or lower Himalayan range.

The Giri river flows along the northern base of the Nahan ridge in its lower course and joins the river Yamuna near Paonta town. Important human settlements which have come up along the Giri river are Yashwantnagar, Dadhau or Renuka and Sataun.

Different types of forests cover the catchment of this river. These include fir, spruce, blue pine, deodar, chir pine, oak, khair and

shisham forests. Major tributaries of the Giri river are--
-- the river Ashni joins it near Sadhupul (Chail)
-- the river Jalal joins it near Dadhau.

A barrage has been constructed across the Giri river at Dadhau. The waters of this river are conducted through an underground channel across the Nahan ridge to the power house at Girinagar. This water is then released into the Bata river.

GIRTHI RIVER

The Girthi river is an important tributary of the Dhauliganga river in Garhwal. It rises from the slopes of the Kungribingri peak situated on the water-divide of Garhwal and Tibet. Thereafter this river descends along a deep gorge having precipitous side walls. From its origin to the Girthi camping ground the valley bottom is broad. It merges directly with the near-vertical side walls having scree slopes on both flanks.

Extremely precipitous side walls occur along this river from Girthi camping ground downstream to Girthi dobhala. Many small amphitheatres are located on the eastern slopes of the Girthi catchment. Melt-waters from the glaciers in these amphitheatres merge with the mainstream of the Girthi river.

The side walls of the valley change from steep to gentle near Baramantia. Small tributary streams drain into the Girthi river at various places. These include--
-- the Kio Gad stream rises in the Laptal area. It merges with the Girthi near Kambhanagar
-- the Choubag Gad is another snow-fed tributary of the Girthi river. It merges with the mainstream in its lower course.

The valley becomes wide and the gradient gentle in the lower course of the Girthi river. It flows into the Dhauliganga river near Kailashpur.

Alpine and sub-alpine vegetation is found in the middle and lower valleys of this river while the upper tracts are under a permanent cover of snow. Small human settlements have come up along the river. These include Girthi dobhala and Kambhanagar.

GOLA RIVER

This is a small spring-fed river of the foothills of Kumaun. It drains the Siwalik hills to the east of Haldwani. This river rises from a small spring in the lower Himalaya. Thereafter it flows towards south-east turns, towards south-west and is joined by another spring-fed tributary flowing in from the west parts of its catchment. Downstream of this confluence, the Gola river takes a U-turn, flows for a short distance in a westerly direction before turning towards south-east and entering the plains.

The upper course of the Gola river flows along a steep gradient. It has cut a gorge across the Siwalik hills. The entire catchment is affected by various levels of accelerated erosion. Sub-tropical pine and deciduous forests are found in the upper and middle catchment of this river. Sal and riverine forests occur along its lower course. These forests are under a heavy biotic pressure.

GORIGANGA RIVER

The Goriganga river is an important right bank tributary of the Kali river draining northern Kumaun. It rises from near Unta Dhura on the Alaknanda-Kali water-divide. This is a snow-fed river whose upper catchment consists of a glaciated terrain. It flows along a south-easterly course and joins the Kali river near Jauljibi.

This river flows along a V-shaped valley in its middle and lower courses. It is joined by a number of snow and rain-fed tributaries coming in from the NE and SW. The gradient of the upper course of this river is very steep. Gradually it becomes gentler near its mouth.

River terraces formed by deposits brought down by running water occur on either banks of this river. Other prominent geomorphic features found in the middle and lower catchment include incised meanders, gorges, rock benches, steep cliffs and waterfalls.

Forests of varying composition and types occur in the catchment of the river Goriganga. These range from the alpine meadows below Unta Dhura to sub-alpine, temperate and sub-tropical coniferous and deciduous forests.

Important human settlements that have come up along the Goriganga river are Milam, Lilam and Jauljibi.

GURTANG RIVER

The river Gurtang is a tributary of the Indus river in Ladakh region of Jammu and Kashmir. It rises from a glacier on the southern slopes of the Ladakh range. Thereafter it flows down to the Indus valley to join it at an elevation of about 4200 metres.

Glaciers have shaped the entire catchment of the river Gurtang. The prominent geomorphic features include hanging valleys, amphitheatres, glacial depressions, lateral and terminal moraines and cirques. The river has a very steep gradient from its source to its confluence with the Indus river.

The entire tract is devoid of a vegetative cover. This is attributed to the high elevation and its situation in the rain-shadow of the main Himalayan range. No human habitation is found along the river Gurtang though its valley is occasionally visited by migratory graziers and travellers moving along the Indus river.

HA CHU RIVER

The Ha Chu river is a tributary of the Raidak river in west-central Bhutan. The source of this river is a valley glacier tennated in a cirque on the south-facing slopes of the main Himalaya. The main channel is joined by a number of smaller streams flowing in from glaciers in hanging valleys. The Ha Chu river then flows in a general direction towards south-south-east to join the Raidak river at Chukho.

The upper valley of Ha Chu river is glaciated while it flows along a deep V-shaped valley in its middle and lower course. There are many rocky outcrops along this river.

Bulk of the Ha Chu catchment is under alpine, sub-alpine and temperate mixed coniferous forests. Ha is a large village that has come up along this river.

HANLE RIVER

The river Hanle is a short left bank tributary of the Indus river. It rises in the snowy wastes on the northern slopes of the Zaskar range in eastern Ladakh of Jammu and Kashmir state. Two feeder streams emanating from glaciers join to form the mainstream of the Hanle river. One flows in from the east while the other comes from the west. The mainstream follows a NNW course and joins the river Indus near Loma.

The Hanle river drains the area to the east of lake Tso Morari in Rupshu. The action of glaciers has played a dominant role in shaping the topography of the catchment of this river. The principal geomorphic features include hanging valleys, moraines and glacial lakes. This river may flood its banks in late summer afternoons.

The vegetative cover in this tract is very scanty. A poor growth of grass comes up between May and September in moist shady depressions. The rest of the catchment is devoid of vegetation. There is virtually no human habitation in this tract. Shepherd and other grazier communities occasionally visit the Hanle valley.

HARLA RIVER

This is a small tributary of the river Beas. It rises as a small channel from the snows in the depressions of the north-western flank of Kulu valley in Himachal Pradesh. This river flows towards SW and merges with the Beas river near Bhuntar, a little upstream of where the main river has cut a gorge across the Dhauladhar range.

The Harla river has a small catchment in the form of a narrow V-shaped valley. The main geomorphic features include steep slopes, cliffs, hanging valleys, terraces and incised meanders. A large part of this tract is covered by fir, spruce, deodar, blue pine, chir pine and oak forests.

Numerous small tributary streams join the river Harla. These are fed by snow that accumulates in the depressions at higher elevations for a large part of the year and the reservoir of underground water which supplies water to small springs all round the year.

Human habitation has come up along this river at many places. The river terraces are under cultivation. A large settlement exists near the confluence of this river with the river Beas.

HOM GADHERA RIVER

The Hom Gadhera river is an important tributary of the Push-pawati or Bhyundar river system that drains the north-eastern part of the Alaknanda catchment. The valley formed by this river lies between Bamai Khal in the north and the Dhauliganga river in the south. Its eastern boundary is formed by the flank of the Barmal peak that descends down to Dhauli near Dhak village. In the west lies the ridge that connects the Jawari kharak and Farsan bank. It separates the catchments of the rivers Kagbhusandi and Hom Gadhera.

This river rises from a hanging glacier tenanted in the cirque of the Barmal peak. Thereafter it descends along a steep gradient along a deep gorge. The slope is precipitous except for the west-facing slope. Many small snow-fed tributaries rise from the eastern slopes of the catchment and drain into the main river.

Alpine, sub-alpine and temperate forests are found in the catchment of this river. Amongst the small settlements that have come up along this river are Painka and Aira.

HUGHE RIVER

The Hughe river is a tributary of the Shyok river which in turn drains into the Indus river. It rises from the snowy wastes of the Gasherbrum glacier. Two main channels from different flanks of this glacier merge after about 1 km to form the mainstream of the Hughe river. Then this river flows towards SSE before it is joined by the Saltoro river draining the eastern flank of its catchment. The Hughe river merges with the Shyok a short distance downstream of its confluence with the Saltoro near Khapalu village.

This river flows along a NNW-SSE direction, straight but wide U-shaped valley. Two offshoots of the Karakoram range form its flanks. Their tops are covered with snow and small glaciers are located in numerous cirques. The melt-waters from these ranges empty themselves into the river Hughe. The valley bottom is flat while its sides are very steep. Thick fluvio-glacial deposits are found on the valley floor. The river flows over a series of rapids.

There is virtually no vegetation in this area. Human population is very scarce though travellers occasionally visit the Hughe catchment.

HUNZA RIVER

The river Hunza rises as the Khunjerab from a glacier north of the Korakoram range in the north-north-western part of Jammu and Kashmir. Thereafter it flows towards SE and cuts across the Karakoram range through a spectacular gorge. Downstream of this gorge the Hunza river follows a SW direction in its middle course. Then it cuts across an offshoot of the Karakoram range and changes its course to SE once again in its lower reaches to finally merge with the Gilgit a little upstream of Bunji where the latter river too empties itself into the Indus.

The main tributaries and feeder streams of the river Hunza are--
-- the river Khunjerab which is its headwaters
-- the river Chapursain rising from a glacier from its north-western flank
-- the river Ghujerab which drains its north-eastern flank
-- the river Shimshal which is a left bank tributary of the river Hunza.

All the above four rivers join the Hunza in its upper course. Small streams flow into this river in its middle and lower courses.

The upper catchment of this river has largely been influenced by the action of glaciers. It flows along a V-shaped valley in its middle course. The Hunza valley opens up in the lower reaches of the river. Small terraces occur on either sides. There is virtually no vegetative cover in any part of the Hunza valley. Human habitation is very sparse.

INDRAVATI RIVER

The Indravati river is a tributary of the Kosi river system that drains eastern Nepal. It rises from the south-facing slopes of the main Himalayan range. The catchment of this river extends from the eastern rim of the Kathmandu basin to the Indravati-Sun Kosi water-divide. This river drains the eastern slopes of the Kathmandu basin.

The Indrawati river drops over a steep gradient. There occur a series of large rapids in its upper course. The steep to precipitous slopes of the valley virtually terminate on the waters' edge. Huge unsorted rock masses and boulders cover the valley bottom. The water flows past interlocking spurs.

Wide terraces have been formed along the lower course of this river. These are under cultivation. Alpine, sub-alpine and temperate forests occur at various elevations in the Indravati catchment. Small villages have come up along its middle and lower courses.

INDUS RIVER

The river Indus rises near Mansarovar lake in the Tibetan plateau. It enters the Himalaya in south-eastern Ladakh near its confluence with the river Gurtang at an elevation of 4200 metres. Thereafter it follows a NNW course between the towering Ladakh range in the north and the Zaskar range in the south. The river has a steep gradient and the valley is very narrow in this tract.

This river makes a sharp turn south of Pangong lake and cuts through the Ladakh range. Further downstream the river turns towards south and rounds the western flank of the Nanga Parbat massif to take a westerly course and leave the Himalaya near Sazin.

The main tributaries of this river in Ladakh region of Jammu and Kashmir are--

-- the river Hanle drains the area to the east of Morari lake and joins the Indus near Loma
-- the Gurtang river joins it near its entry point into Ladakh
-- the river Zaskar drains the northern slopes of the Zaskar range and the main Himalaya. It joins the Indus about 40 kms below Leh

- the river Shigar (south) merges with the Indus at Marol
- the Shigar river flows into the Indus at Skardu
- the Shyok river joins the Indus river about 40 kms upstream of Skardu
- the Gilgit river joins the river Indus at Bunji
- the Astor river joins the Indus a short distance downstream of Bunji.

A number of human settlements lie along the river Indus in Ladakh. These include Leh, Marol, Skardu and Bunji.

Flash floods are known to have occurred in the Indus basin from time to time. The most devastating flood took place in the latter part of the last century when a dam formed by an avalanche burst in the Indus catchment of Ladakh. Huge loss of life and property occurred.

INDUS RIVER SYSTEM

The drainage basin of the Indus river system extends from the Nanga Parbat massif in the extreme north-western part of the country to the western slopes of the Shimla ridge in Himachal Pradesh. It includes the whole of Jammu and Kashmir and most of Himachal Pradesh. The extreme northern tract of the Indus basin consists of the cold deserts of Ladakh, Lahul, Spiti and Pooh. South of this tract lies the higher Himalayan mountain wall. The middle and lower Himalaya occupy the central part of the Indus basin. The low rolling Siwalik hills occur along its southern periphery.

Climatic conditions vary from arctic in areas above an elevation of about 4000 metres to sub-tropical in the southern hills. The cold desert areas are virtually devoid of rainfall. Kashmir too does not receive rain from the SW monsoons. Very heavy snowfall occurs at elevations of over 2000 metres.

Besides the Indus river, other important rivers of this system are--
- the river Satluj and its tributaries draining parts of Himachal Pradesh
- the river Beas and its tributaries draining parts of Himachal Pradesh
- the river Ravi and its tributaries draining parts of Himachal Pradesh
- the river Chenab and its tributaries draining parts of Himachal Pradesh and Jammu and Kashmir
- the river Jhelum and its tributaries draining parts of Jammu and Kashmir.

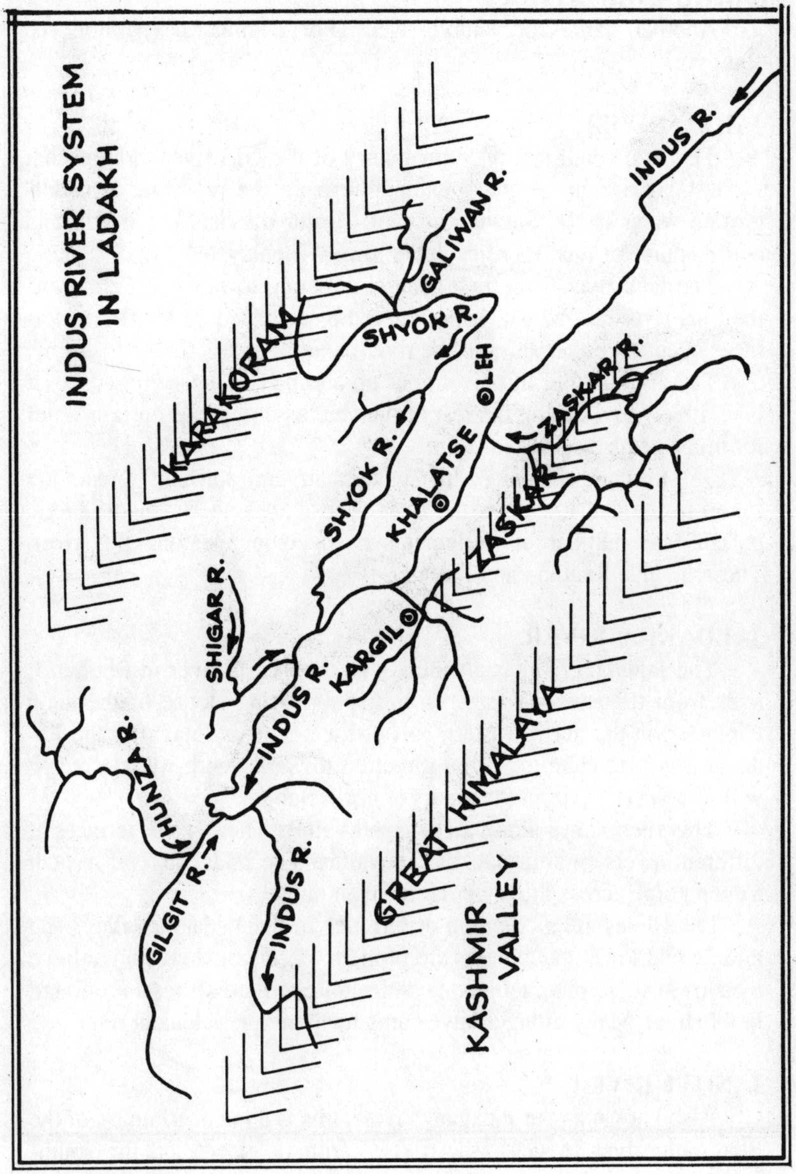
INDUS RIVER SYSTEM
IN LADAKH
KARAKORAM
SHYOK R.
GALIWAN R.
SHYOK R.
LEH
KHALATSE
ZASKAR R.
ZASKAR
INDUS R.
SHIGAR R.
INDUS R.
KARGIL
HUNZA R.
GILGIT R.
INDUS R.
GREAT HIMALAYA
KASHMIR
VALLEY

JADHGANGA RIVER

Another name for Janhvi river. (For detailed description see 'Janhvi river').

JALAL RIVER

This is a small spring-fed tributary of the Giri river in Himachal Pradesh. It rises as a spring emanating from the reservoir of underground water in the Sarahan area of Sirmur district. The origin and entire course of this river lies in the lower Himalaya.

The Jalal river flows in a general direction towards east and joins the Giri river at Dadhau. It has carved a V-shaped valley. River terraces occur on either sides of the river bank.

The discharge of this river goes up abruptly in the rainy season. It is relatively low during the rest of the year as it depends on rain water for much of its discharge.

Sub-tropical chir pine, ban oak, khair and shisham forests are found in the catchment of this river. These are under a severe biotic pressure. A number of settlements have come up along this river. These include Bagthan and Dadhau.

JALDAKHA RIVER

The Jaldakha river is a tributary of the Teesta river in Bhutan. It rises from the snowy wastes on the south-facing slopes of the main Himalaya in the north-western part of the country. Thereafter the Jaldakha river flows in a general direction towards south-west to merge with the Teesta river in the plains of north Bengal.

This river flows along a U-shaped valley. There occur terraces at different levels on both flanks of its valley. The Jaldakha river has cut a deep gorge across the lower Himalayan range.

Landslides are a common occurrence in the Jaldakha valley. The middle and lower catchments are prone to accelerated erosion. Alpine meadows, sub-alpine, temperate and semi-evergreen forests are found in this tract. Many villages have come up along the Jaldakha river.

JANHVI RIVER

Also known as the Jadhganga river, this is a major tributary of the Bhagirathi river in Garhwal. It rises from a glacier on the south-western slopes of the main Himalaya in Uttarkashi district. This river flows into the Bhagirathi river upstream of Uttarkashi.

The upper reaches of this river flow along a glaciated valley.

Thereafter it flows through a V-shaped valley that is lined by rows of terraces. The main geomorphic features include incised meanders and rock benches. Alpine, sub-alpine and temperate forests occur in the catchment of this river. A number of villages exist along the Janhvi river.

JANTI GAD RIVER

This is a tributary of the Dhauliganga river in Garhwal. It rises from the slopes of the Kalajabra-Chorhoti peak and drains into the mainstream near Ghamsali.

JHELUM RIVER

The river Jhelum is the westernmost of the five major tributaries of the river Indus system. It rises from the northern slopes of the Pir Panjal range which girdles the famous Kashmir valley. Thereafter it slowly winds its way across the flat valley in a general north-westerly direction before cutting across the Pir Panjal range through a gorge at Baramulla. Thereafter it flows towards west to join the Chenab.

The upper course of this river is fed by small deposits of ice and snow in the depressions of the Pir Panjal range. The northern slopes of this mountain range are covered by sub-alpine and temperate forests.

The Jhelum enters the flat Kashmir valley in its middle course. Its speed becomes very slow and the river meanders across the valley, past the town of Srinagar where houseboats and shikaras ply on this river. As a matter of fact the river is a part and parcel of the lives of Kashmiris. It flows across the foothills in its lower course where the gradient is once again steep.

The main tributaries of the river Jhelum are--
-- the Liddar river which drains Pahalgam area and joins the river Jhelum near Anantnag
-- the river Sind which rises from the southern slopes of the main Himalaya and merges with the Jhelum near Srinagar
-- the river Kishenganga which merges with the Jhelum in the foothills.

Important human settlements that have come up among this river are Anantnag, Srinagar, Ganderbal and Baramulla.

KAFNI RIVER

The river Kafni is a small snow-fed tributary of the Pindar river in Garhwal. It rises from the snowy wastes of the Kafni glacier which

JHELUM RIVER SYSTEM IN KASHMIR VALLEY

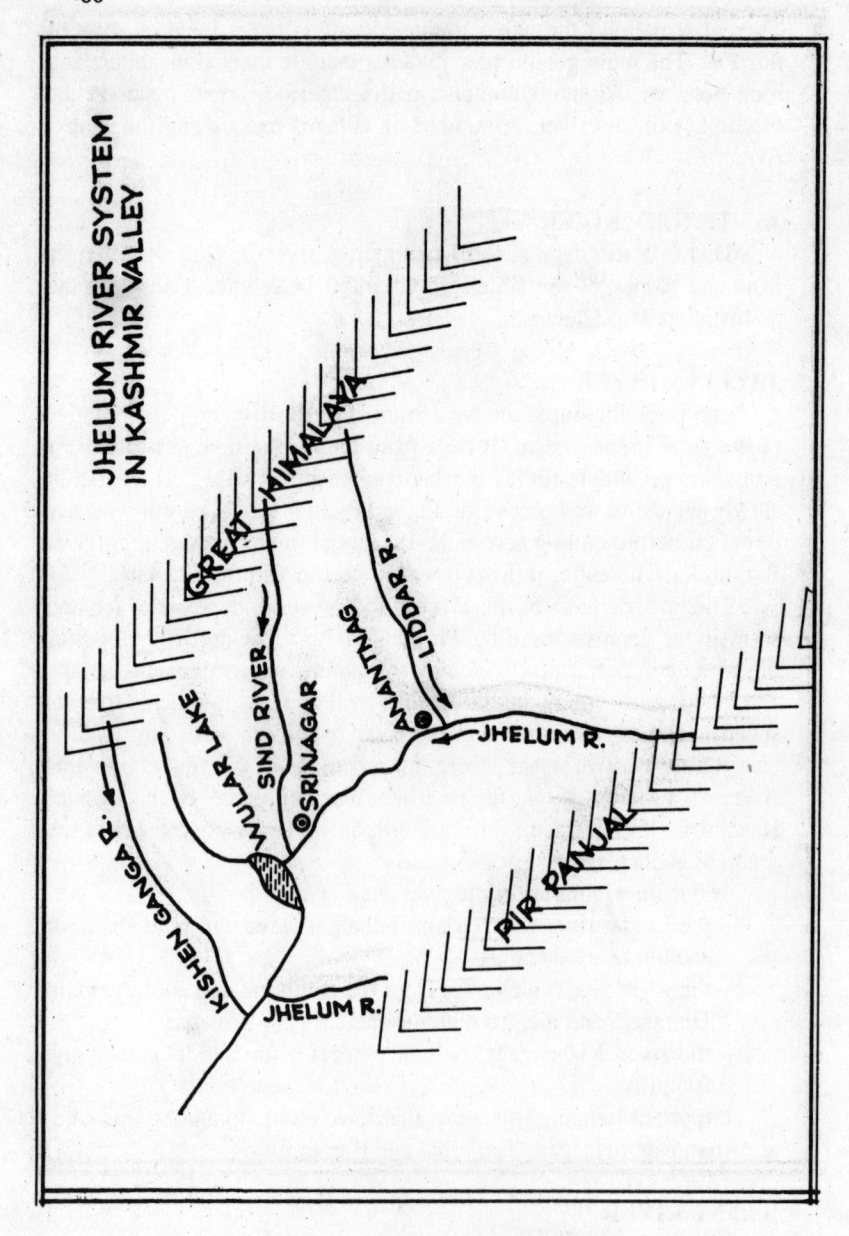

extends for about 3 kms from the source of the river and fills the breadth of the valley. The mainstream emanating from this glacier is joined by two small tributaries, one flowing in from the west and the other from the east. A huge terminal moraine has been deposited in this glacial valley.

The upper course of the Kafni river flows along a U-shaped valley. Steep walls rise from either sides of the broad valley bottom. Numerous meadows line the river in its upper course. There is a general change in the terrain lower down. The valley becomes narrow and a deep gorge has developed. River terraces occur near the confluence of this river with the Pindar at Dwali.

Moist alpine and sub-alpine vegetation is found in the Kafni catchment. The rest of the area is under a permanent cover of snow. The meadows are frequented by graziers during the summer months. Small villages exist along the lower course of the Kafni river.

KAGBHUSAND RIVER

This is a snow-fed tributary of the river Pushpawati or Bhyundar. It originates as small mainstreams each draining away the waters of a trough glacier. The trunk glacier lies in a trough at the base of Barmal Dhar while the tributary glaciers feeding this river descend from Dhanesh Parbat, Oti-ka-danda in the east and Kankul Khal in the west. This river joins the Pushpawati or Bhyundar river at Bhyundar a little downstream of the Valley of Flowers.

The valley of the Kagbhusand river is surrounded in the northeast and south by many pyramidal peaks, viz small snow-clad peaks on the truncated spur of the Gauri Parbat lying along east-west in the north, Gauri Parbat, Hathi Parbat and Dhanesh Parbat in the east and Barmal in the south.

The entire catchment of this river shows evidences of extensive glaciation. A part of its discharge comes from the Kaghusand tal, a glacial lake located in the cirque of the Kankul Khal. Many small snow-fed streams drain into this river at various places.

Vast alpine meadows are found in the upper catchment of this river. These are visited by migratory herds of sheep and goats during the summer months. Sub-alpine and temperate forests are found in its middle and lower reaches.

KAKRA GAD RIVER

This is a small spring-fed tributary of the Mandakini river in

Garhwal. It flows into the mainstream at the mountain hamlet of Kakra in Chamoli district.

KALAPANI RIVER

This river is the eastern headwaters of the Kali river near the Nepal-Kumaun border. It is made up of numerous small springs fed by underground waters.

KALI RIVER

The river Kali or Kaliganga drains eastern Kumaun and western Nepal. It flows for a considerable distance along the border of Kumaun (India) and Nepal. This river is formed after the confluence of two main headwaters--
- --the river Kalapani is its eastern headwaters. It is made up of numerous small springs fed by underground waters
- --the river Kuthi Yankti forms the western headwaters of the river Kali. It rises in the snow-fields of the Himadri on the southern slopes of the great or main Himalayan range.

Both these headwaters join to form the Kali at the base of the main Himalayan range. Thereafter the river flows in a SSW direction along a deep V-shaped valley to enter the plains of northern India at Baramdeo. It flows into the Ghagra in the plains of Bihar where this river is also known as the Sarda.

The valley of this river is steep. River terraces of various sizes occur along it. Other geomorphic features include incised meanders, ridges, spurs and waterfalls. Important tributaries of the Kali river are--
- -- the river Dhauliganga draining north-eastern Kumaun
- -- the river Goriganga draining north-central Kumaun
- -- the river Sarju draining central Kumaun
- -- the river Ladhiya draining south-central Kumaun

Some human settlements that have come up along this river are Lipulekh, Garbyang, Dharchula, Jauljibi and Tanakpur.

KALI GANDAKI RIVER

Another name for the Krishna Gandaki or Gandak river that drains central Nepal. (For detailed description see 'Gandak river').

KALIGANGA RIVER

Another name for the Kali river which drains eastern Kumaun

and western Nepal. (For detailed description see 'Kali river').

KAMENG RIVER

The Kameng is an important river of western Arunachal Pradesh. It rises in the snows of the Kangto group of peaks which are a part of the main Himalayan range along the border with Tibet. In its upper course the Kameng river flows in a south-easterly direction between two towering ridges. The upper catchment consists of a deep, V-shaped valley. Terraces have formed along the river.

The river turns towards east in the area to the east of Bomdila. The valley is more open in its middle course. In its lower reaches the river Kameng takes a wide U-turn between the foothills and joins the Brahmaputra river opposite Silghat in Assam.

Dense forests are found in the Kameng valley. These range from the alpine pastures in the upper tracts to dense evergreen forests in the foothills. Many human settlements have come up in the Kameng valley. These include Riang, Bomdila and Charduar.

Important tributaries of the river Kameng are--

-- the river Bichom draining north-western Arunachal

-- the river Tenga draining north-western Arunachal.

KAMET RIVER

This is a small tributary of the Dhauliganga river. It has a delta-shaped catchment with its apex near Shepuk. The Kamet river is formed by three large streams rising from the Uttar Paikana, Raikana and Purbi Kamet glaciers. These channels merge to form the main stream. The Kamet valley is bound by a jagged-shaped ridge having a number of peaks. It joins the Dhauliganga river near Geldhung.

The upper tracts are under a permanent cover of snow. Alpine, sub-alpine and temperate vegetation is found in the middle and lower catchments of this river.

KAMLA RIVER

This is a large tributary of the Subansiri river that drains central Arunachal Pradesh. It rises as three main channels from small glaciers on the main Himalaya near the Indo-Tibetan border. The Kamla river flows in a general direction towards south-west and joins the Subansiri river near Leling.

Numerous tributaries flow into the Kamla river. Its largest feeder is the Kurung river. Their confluence is near Par.

The Kamla river flows between towering mountains. It has carved incised meanders and terraces in its course to the Subansiri. The entire catchment of this river bears thick forests. Niktak, Par, Hachi, Onga and Gocham are some villages along this river.

KARNALI RIVER

The Karnali river is the longest tributary of the Gandak basin which drains western Nepal. The mainstream of this river rises in the springs of Mapcha Chungo in Tibet near the Mansarovar lake. It flows in a south-east direction and crosses into Nepal through a spectacular gorge across the main Himalayan range near Simikot. The region is known as Humla and consists of high peaks including the Api and Nampe.

The Karnali flows towards west along the lower Himalaya or Mahabharat Lekh, then turns and cuts a gorge through this mountain barriers. It then flows through the foothills as the Ghagra and enters the plains.

The main tributaries of the Karnali river are--
-- a snow-fed stream rising in Tibet joins the Karnali river west of Simikot
-- the Panjang river rises from near Charkabhotgaon and joins the Karnali river near Phijorgaon
-- the Seti is an important western tributary of the Karnali river. It merges with the mainstream just south of the Mahabharat Lekh
-- the Bheri river drains the Dhaulagiri Himal massif. It flows into the Karnali near the Mahabharat Lekh gorge.
-- the Chauka river merges with the Karnali river in the foothills.

In its course through Nepal, the Karnali river has formed a V-shaped valley. It has cut gorges across the mountains that impede its southward bound course.

The entire catchment of this river bears rich forests. These vary from dry and moist alpine meadows to temperate and sub-tropical forests. The vegetation of the lower hills is under intense biotic pressure. Among the important settlements that have come up along this river are Simikot and Dailekh.

KAURIALA RIVER

The Kauriala river is a small rain-fed Siwalik tributary of the Ghagra river in Nepal. It rises on the south-facing slopes of the lower Himalaya. Thereafter this river flows in a general direction towards

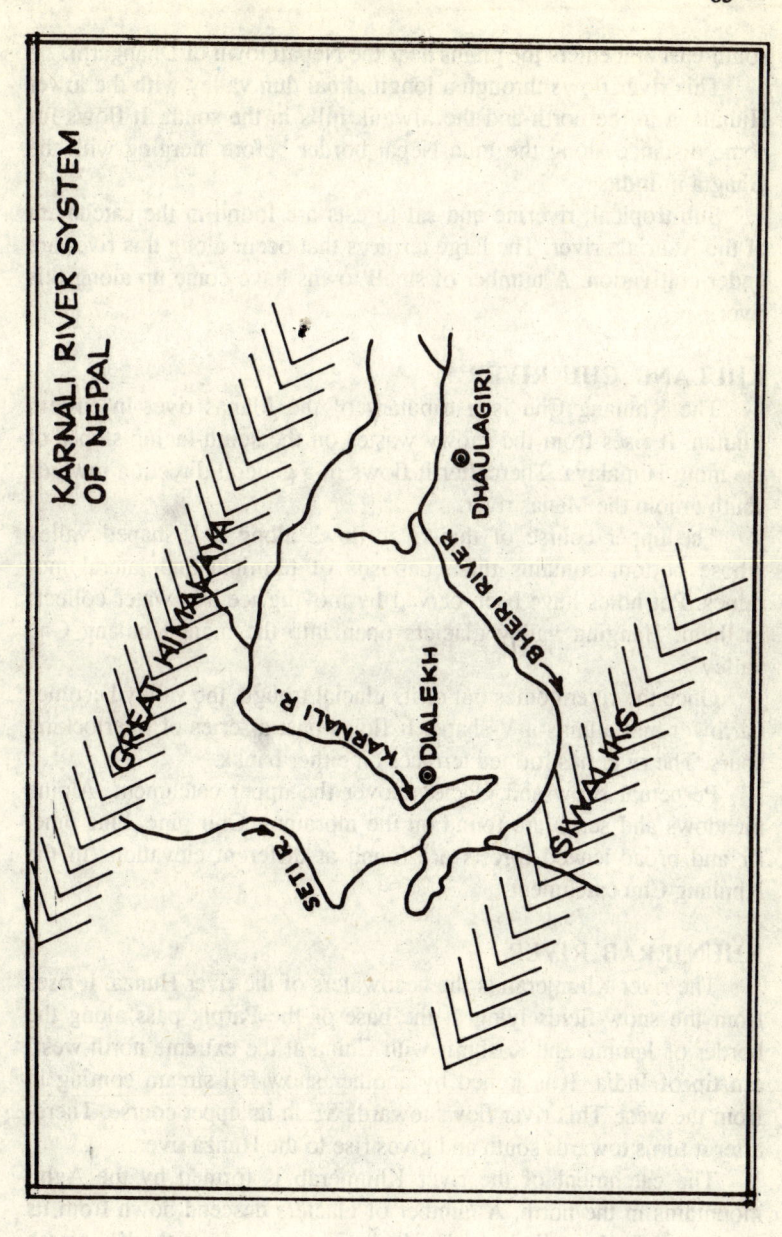

KARNALI RIVER SYSTEM OF NEPAL

DHAULAGIRI

GREAT HIMALAYA

BHERI RIVER

KARNALI R.

DIALEKH

SIWALIKS

SETI R.

south-east and enters the plains near the Nepali town of Dhangarhi.

This river flows through a longitudinal dun valley with the lower Himalaya in the north and the Siwalik hills in the south. It flows for some distance along the Indo-Nepal border before merging with the Ghagra in India.

Sub-tropical, riverine and sal forests are found in the catchment of the Kauriala river. The large terraces that occur along this river are under cultivation. A number of small towns have come up along this river.

KHULANG CHU RIVER

The Khulang Chu is a tributary of the Manas river in eastern Bhutan. It rises from the snowy wastes on the south-facing slopes of the main Himalaya. Thereafter it flows in a general direction towards south to join the Manas river.

The upper course of this river flows along a U-shaped valley whose bottom contains thick deposits of terminal and lateral moraines. Pot holes have been carved by moving ice and water collects in them. Hanging valley glaciers open into the main Khulang Chu valley.

Once the river comes out of its glacial trough, the valley becomes narrower and attains a V-shape. It flows past a series of interlocking spurs. The river has formed terraces on either banks.

Perpetual snow and glaciers cover the upper catchment. Alpine meadows and scrub are found on the moraines. Chir pine, blue pine, fir and broad-leaved forests are found at different elevations in the Khulang Chu catchment.

KHUNJERAB RIVER

The river Khunjerab is the headwaters of the river Hunza. It rises from the snow-fields lying at the base of the Parpik pass along the border of Jammu and Kashmir with China at the extreme north-western tip of India. It is joined by another snow-fed stream coming in from the west. This river flows towards SE in its upper course. Thereafter it turns towards south and gives rise to the Hunza river.

The catchment of the river Khunjerab is formed by the Aghil mountains in the north. A number of glaciers descend down from its slopes and feed small channels which combine to form the Khunjerab or the mainstream of the river Hunza. The main geomorphic features include hanging valleys, waterfalls, glaciers, snow-fields, lateral and terminal moraines and cirques.

The entire tract is devoid of a vegetative cover as the altitude and climatic conditions do not permit anything to grow there. There are no human settlements in the catchment of the river Khunjerab.

KHURANA RIVER

The river Khurana is a tributary of the Zaskar river which in turn drains into the Indus near Leh in Jammu and Kashmir. This river rises from the snowy wastes at the base of the northern slopes of the Zaskar range in south-eastern Ladakh in the area to the east of Markha.

Thereafter the Khurana river flows towards north-west to join the Zaskar in the area to the north-west of Markha. It flows in a valley between the Zaskar range in the west and its offshoot in the east. Markha is located on this offshoot range.

The entire catchment of this river has been shaped by the action of glaciers and running water. Its upper valley is U-shaped and was perhaps covered by a glacier in the past. Moraines laid down by glaciers are found in this valley. Waterfalls occur in the side valleys of the river Khurana.

Alpine meadows are found in the depressions. The rest of the valley is largely devoid of a vegetative cover as it lies in the rain-shadow of the main Himalayan range. Human habitation is very sparse.

KIO GAD RIVER

This is a tributary of the Girthi river in Garhwal. It rises in the Laptal area and merges with the Girthi river near Kambhanagar.

KISHENGANGA RIVER

The river Kishenganga is an important tributary of the Jhelum river. It rises from the southern slopes of the main Himalayan range near Sonmarg on the north-western fringe of Kashmir valley. This river flows towards NW in its upper and middle courses. Thereafter it takes a U-turn and flows towards SE to join the Jhelum at Muzaffarabad.

The upper catchment of river Kishenganga consists of steep slopes, razor-sharp ridges and hanging valleys. The river flows along a very steep gradient in this tract. Its speed slows down once it enters the flat, open Kashmir valley. This river then drains the north-western fringe of the valley.

It cuts across the Pir Panjal range through a gorge near Tithwal. The Kishenganga river is joined by many small, snow-fed tributary streams, particularly from the mountains lying along the north-western fringe of the Kashmir valley.

Dense coniferous and broad-leaved forests are found in the catchment of this river. Alpine meadows occur near Sonmarg. The area along both banks of this river are under cultivation in the Kashmir valley. Important human settlements that have come up along this river are Keran, Tithwal and Muzaffarabad.

KNOH RIVER

This is a small river of the Siwalik or outer Himalayan tract of the U.P. hills. It is fed by underground water and rises on the outer Himalayan slopes. Thereafter this river flows in a general direction towards south to enter the plains of western Uttar Pradesh.

Dry sub-tropical and riverine forests are found along the Knoh river. These are under a heavy biotic pressure. The entire catchment of this river is subject to accelerated erosion. Flash floods commonly occur during the rainy season.

KOMA CHU RIVER

This is an important tributary of the Kuru river in Bhutan. It merges with the mainstream near Lhuntsi. The upper catchment of this river is glaciated.

KOSI (KUMAUN) RIVER

The Kosi river is an important river of the foothills of Kumaun. It rises as two spring-fed channels in the lower Himalaya near Almora. The two channels merge after a short distance and the Kosi river flows in a general direction towards south-west before making a U-turn and flowing in a south-easterly direction and entering the plains of western Uttar Pradesh.

A number of small tributaries flow into the Kosi river at various places from its source to where it enters the plains.

This river has carved a deep V-shaped gully. Other geomorphic features of the Kosi catchment are incised meanders, interlocking spurs, river terraces at various levels, ridges, rock benches and cliffs.

Small islands have formed at the confluence of the Kosi with its tributaries. It has cut deep gorges through the lower Himalaya and Siwalik hills.

Temperate and sub-tropical coniferous and deciduous forests are found in the catchment of the river Kosi. Khair and shisham forests occur along the river bed. A number of human settlements have come up along this river. Amongst these are Garjia and Ramnagar.

KOSI RIVER SYSTEM

The Kosi or Sapt Kosi river system drains eastern Nepal. It is known as the Sapt Kosi because of the seven rivers which join together in east-central Nepal to form this river. The main rivers forming the Kosi sytsem are--

-- the river Sun Kosi which rises as a number of snow-fed streams beyond the Gosainthan massif
-- the Indravati river which drains the eastern outer rim of the Kathmandu valley
-- the Bhola Kosi which drains the snow-melt waters of the Cho-Oyu and the Gauri Shankar massifs
-- the Dudh Kosi which drains the Mt. Everest massif, the highest group of peaks in the world
-- the river Arun which rises in the trans-Himalayan zone of Tibet. It has cut a spectacular gorge across the main Himalayan range to the east of the Mt. Everest massif
-- the river Barun which rises from the Barun glacier at the base of Mt. Makalu, the fourth highest peak in the world
-- the river Tamur which is the easternmost tributary of the river Kosi. It rises from the snows on the western flank of the Kanchanjunga group of peaks.

The combined river Kosi or Sapt Kosi then flows towards south to emerge from the hills through the Chatra gorge.

KRISHNA GANDAKI RIVER

This is the mainstream of the Gandak river that drains central Nepal. It rises near Mustang Bhot in the trans-Himalayan tract in Tibet. Thereafter the river enters Nepal. The Krishna Gandaki is commonly known as the Gandak river in its middle and lower courses. (For detailed description see 'Gandak river').

KULONG RIVER

The Kulong river drains the extreme north-eastern part of Bhutan. It rises as two mainstreams from glaciers on the main Himalaya near the border of Bhutan and Tibet. Thereafter this river flows in a gen-

SAPT KOSI RIVER SYSTEM IN NEPAL

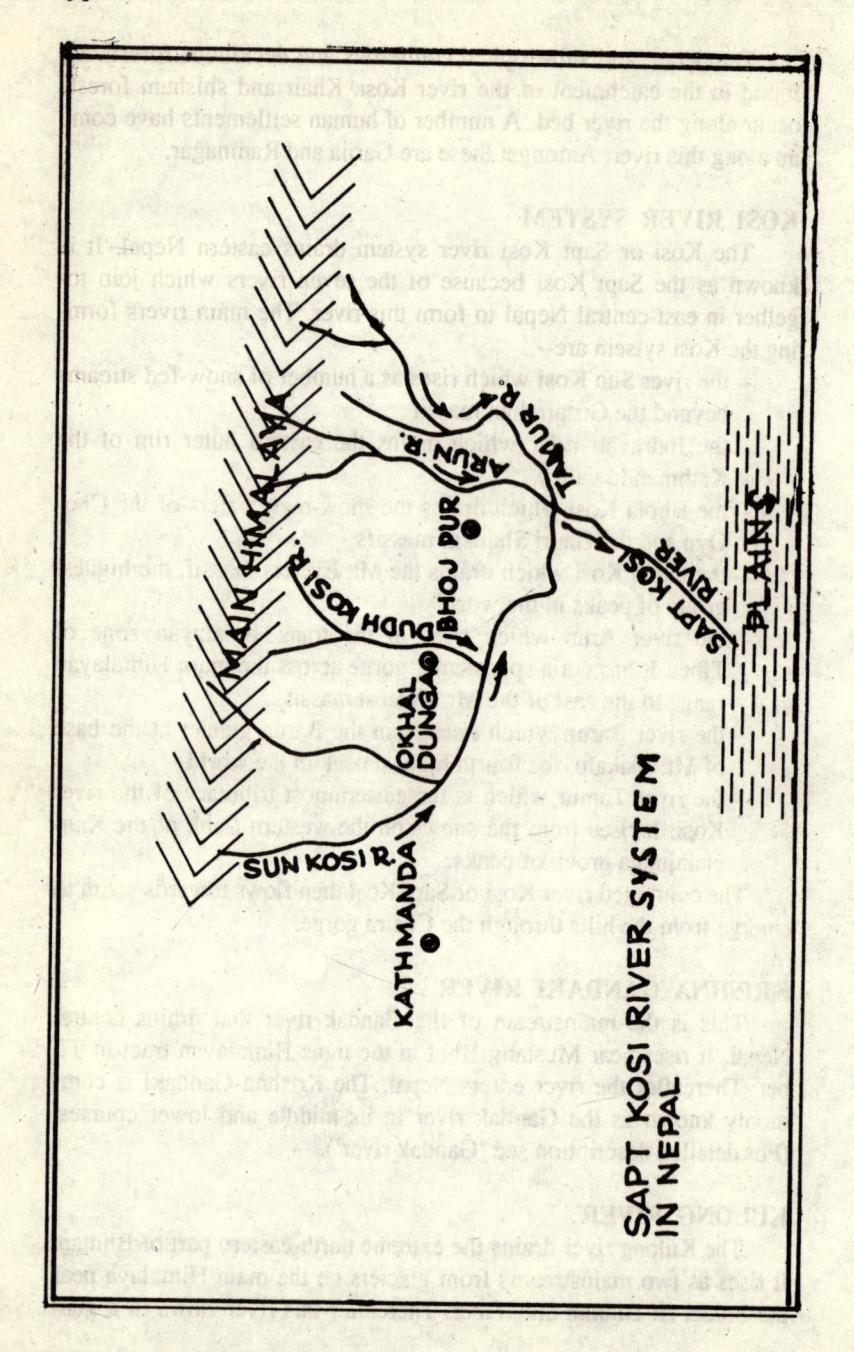

eral direction towards south to enter the main channel of the Manas river.

This river flows along a deep V-shaped valley lined by river-cut and river-built terraces. There occur dense forests in the catchment of this river. Tashi Yangtsi Dzong is the principal human settlement that has come up along this river.

KURU RIVER

The Kuru river is an important tributary of the Manas river. It drains a part of eastern Bhutan. The mainstream of the Kuru river originates in Tibet. This river has cut a deep gorge across the main Himalayan range. It flows in a general direction towards south, then turns towards south-south-east before flowing into the Manas river.

The Koma Chu river is a tributary of the Kuru river. These two rivers merge near Lhuntsi.

Glaciers and snow-fields occur on the upper catchment of this river. The snow-melt water merges with the mainstream at various places. The upper valley has been carved by the action of glaciers. The valley bottom is strewn with moraines on which alpine meadows are growing.

Temperate blue pine and broad-leaved forests occur in the middle and lower valley of this river. A part of the catchment is under cultivation.

KURUNG RIVER

The Kurung river drains central Arunachal Pradesh. It rises from the snowy wastes of the south-facing slopes of the main Himalaya on the Indo-Tibetan border. This river flows in a general direction towards south-west and west to merge with the Kamla river near Par.

Numerous tributaries draining different parts of the Kurung catchment join the mainstream. Its valley bears dense forests. Amongst the settlements that have come up along the Kurung river are Dui Yambi, Takum, Palin and Bindula.

KUTHI YANKTI RIVER

This is the western headwaters of the Kali river near the Nepal-Kumaun Border. It rises in the snowfields of the Himadri on the southern slopes of the great or main Himalayan range.

KWILA GAD RIVER

This is a small tributary of the Lastar Gad river in Tehri district of Garhwal. It is fed by underground water/springs.

LACHUNG RIVER

The river Lachung is a feeder channel of the river Teesta. It rises in a glacier below Paunhri on the main Himalayan mountain wall along the Indo-China border in northern Sikkim. Thereafter the river Lachung flows towards south along the base of an offshoot ridge of the main Himalaya to join the Teesta coming in from the north-west at Lachen.

The upper catchment of the Lachung river is glaciated. Numerous small glaciers descend into the valley from the northern wall. They feed small channels that empty into the river Lachung at different places. The valley attains a V-shape in the middle and lower courses of this river. It opens up near its confluence with the Teesta river. Small river terraces have formed all along the course of this river.

The higher tracts are under a permanent cover of snow. Alpine pastures occur down below. Temperate forests occur at lower elevations. Human habitation is very sparse. Lachen is the largest settlement of the Lachung valley.

LADHIYA RIVER

The river Ladhiya is a small tributary of the Kali river. It rises as two small springs fed by underground water in an area to the NNE of Nainital in Kumaun. This river flows towards SE in its upper and middle courses, turns towards east and flows into the Kali river upstream of Tanakpur.

Two small springs are the headwaters of this river. They rise at a distance of about 20 kms from each other. Thereafter they merge and flow towards east. A number of smaller streams flow into the Ladhiya river, particularly from the northern flank of its valley.

The Ladhiya valley is deep and V-shaped in its upper course but opens up towards its mouth. Many small paired and unpaired terraces occur along the river. These are composed of the deposits laid down by the river over thousands of years. Broad terraces occur near its confluence with the Kali river. Other prominent geomorphic features include incised meanders, ridges and spurs.

Forests of varying types and compositions are found in the catchment of this river. These include both coniferous and deciduous forests. Small villages are located along the Ladhiya river.

LASTAR GAD RIVER

The river Lastar Gad is a major tributary of the Mandakini river which in turn drains into the Alaknanda river at Rudraparyag. This river rises as a spring-fed stream in the mountain slopes to the north of Mayali on the water-divide of the Bhagirathi and Alaknanda in Tehri district of Garhwal. Thereafter it flows towards south in its upper course. This river is joined by many small streams in its upper catchment.

The Lastar Gad river turns towards south-east near Mayali and flows for a considerable distance before joining the Mandakini river near Tilwara. The entire course of this river is along a deep V-shaped valley. The main geomorphic features include incised meanders, rock benches and river-built and river-cut terraces. A large river terrace occurs near the confluence of this river with the Mandakini.

The two prominent tributaries of the Lastar Gad river are the Kwila Gad and Ghengar Khala.

Sub-tropical coniferous and deciduous forests occur in the Lastar Gad catchment. Important human settlements that have come up along its course are Khale, Toneta and Tilwara.

LHONAK RIVER

The river Lhonak is a tributary of the Teesta river. It rises from the snowy wastes of northern Sikkim as a small stream. Thereafter it flows in a general direction towards south and joins the Teesta. The upper catchment of this river has been carved by the action of glaciers. The main Himalayan wall with its towering snow-clad peaks forms the northern boundary of its catchment. Small glaciers or tongues of perpetual ice descend from the depressions between the ridges on the mountain to the valley. They give birth to small streams which join the main channel of the Lhonak river which in turn is fed by a glacier.

The upper course of this river is along an ancient glacial valley while the middle and lower courses have been carved both by the movement of ice in the past and the action of running water. Side valleys formed by snow-melt waters open into the main Lhonak valley at various places.

No vegetation is found in the higher reaches. Alpine pastures occur near the snowline while sub-alpine and temperate forests are found at lower elevations. Human habitation in the Lhonak valley is very sparse. It is visited by graziers.

LIDDAR RIVER

The Liddar river is a tributary of the river Jhelum. It rises from the Chandanwari glacier at the base of Pissoo top on the pilgrim trail to Amarnath in the north-eastern flank of Kashmir valley. It is a small channel in this tract and flows in a south-westerly direction towards the mountain resort of Pahalgam.

Thereafter the river turns towards south-south-west and enters the flat Kashmir valley. It finally merges with the river Jhelum at Anantnag.

The upper course of this river flows through a U-shaped valley carved by an ancient glacier. Snow-fed streams join the Liddar river from both sides. The valley becomes V-shaped downstream of Pahalgam. The gradient of this river is very steep from Chandanwari to a little downstream of Pahalgam. It is considerably reduced once the river enters the flat Kashmir valley near Anantnag.

The main tributary of the Liddar river is the Aru river which originates from the Aru glacier in the north-western part of the Liddar catchment and merges with the mainstream at Pahalgam.

The entire tract is covered by dense alpine, sub-alpine and temperate forests. The towns that have come up along the Liddar river are Chandanwari, Pahalgam and Anantnag.

LIPA RIVER

The Lipa river is an important tributary of the Spiti river which in turn drains into the Satluj river in Himachal Pradesh. The origin of this river is a boulder-strewn glacier in the upper tracts of the Spiti valley. Numerous small channels rise from the glacier and merge to form the mainstream of this river.

This river has carved a U-shaped valley in its upper course which changes to a deep V-shaped gorge in its middle and lower courses. Small terraces occur on either flanks of the Lipa valley.

Dry alpine meadows occur on the moraines. Human habitation is virtually absent.

LOHAWATI RIVER

The Lohawati river is a small tributary of the Kali river. It rises as a stream fed by underground water near Champawat. Thereafter it flows in a south-easterly direction to join the Kali river a short distance upstream of its confluence with the river Ladhiya.

This river flows along a V-shaped valley. It is fed by numerous small water channels that originate from springs formed wherever the ground water table has come in contact with the topographic slope of the land. The valley is narrower in the upper course of the river. It widens towards its confluence with the Kali. The main geomorphic features of the Lohawati valley are paired and unpaired terraces, incised meanders, rock benches, ridges and spurs.

Sub-tropical coniferous and deciduous forests cover the entire tract. They are in a degraded condition due to heavy biotic pressure. Small human settlements have come up along this river.

LOHIT RIVER

The Lohit river is an important tributary of the Brahmaputra river. It rises as two snow-fed mainstreams in the area to the north of the Nyimo Chomo and Niechen Gangri mountains in Tibet. Thereafter these two channels flow in a general direction towards south and merge at Rima to form the Lohit.

This river enters Indian territory near Rima and flows for a considerable distance towards south. It then makes a right angle turn and flows in a north-westerly direction before turning once again towards south. It begins to flow towards west once again near Brahmakund and merges with the Brahmaputra near Sadiya.

Its course through the foothills of Arunachal Pradesh meanders between offshoots of the lower Himalaya. The river straightens out once it enters the Brahmaputra plains. In its middle course it flows along a V-shaped valley and is flanked on both sides by small terraces.

Thick forests cover the entire catchment of the Lohit river in Arunachal Pradesh. These are mainly semi-evergreen and evergreen forests. The main human settlements that have come up along this river are Brahmakund and Lohit.

LUNI RIVER

The river Luni is a small tributary of the river Beas. It rises from the south-facing slopes of the Dhauladhar range in the Kangra valley of Himachal Pradesh. Thereafter it flows towards south to merge with the river Beas in the central part of Kangra valley.

Small feeder channels fed by deposits of ice that remain in the depressions of the towering Dhauladhar range merge to form the river Luni. Its gradient is very steep in the upper tracts when the river descends down the foothills of the Dhauladhar.

There is a marked change in its gradient once the river enters the gently sloping bottom of the Kangra valley. The Luni river begins to meander in its middle and lower courses before it flows into the river Beas.

Forests are found in its upper catchment. However the land along its middle and lower courses is fertile and is being extensively cultivated. Many human settlements have come up along the river Luni.

MADHYAMAHESHWARI RIVER

This is an important tributary of the Mandakini river in the Kedarnath valley of Garhwal. It drains the southern slopes of the imposing Chaukhamba peak. This river rises from Nandikund, a glacial lake tenanted in the easternmost cirque. Thereafter it joins the Mandakini river about 2 kms to the north of Ukhimath.

The gradient in the upper reaches of this river is not very steep. There occur vast undulating alpine meadows in this tract. The river meanders for about 2 kms before descending rapidly through a series of rapids and small waterfalls.

The middle and lower valley of the Madhyamaheshwari river is deep and V-shaped. Terraces occurring at various levels line both the banks of this river near its confluence with the Mandakini.

Small tributaries join the Madhyamaheshwari river at various places. These include--
- -- small channels from valley glaciers drain into the upper course of the Madhyamaheshwari river
- -- the Madhyamaheshwari Gad is a small but important tributary of this river. It rises from a glacier and joins the main river near Madhyamaheshwari temple
- -- the Markanda river joins the river at Bantoli.

Alpine and sub-alpine forests are found in the catchment of the Madhyamaheshwari river. Amongst the main human settlements are Bantoli and Madhyamaheshwari.

MADHYAMAHESHWARI GAD RIVER

Also known as the Madhyamaheshwari nala, this is a tributary of the Madhyamaheshwari river. It rises from a small valley glacier in a cirque near the Nandikund lake. Thereafter this river descends rapidly to join the Madhyamaheshwari river about 2 kms south of Madhyamaheshwari temple.

The valley of this river is U-shaped and has been carved by the action of glaciers. Small channels from glaciers in the adjoining hanging valleys open into the main valley of this river. It descends through a series of rapids to its mouth. The valley bottom is strewn with striated boulders. There also occur moraine deposits in this tract.

The upper catchment of this river is devoid of a vegetative cover. Alpine meadows are found on the moraines. Other forests found in this area include sub-alpine and temperate vegetation. Small settlements have come up along the lower course of this river.

MALUNG RIVER

The Malung river is a glacial torrent of the trans-Himalayan tract of Lahul and Spiti in Himachal Pradesh. It rises from a valley glacier on the northern slopes of the main Himalayan range in the area of the north-west of Hansi. The Malung river flows towards north in its upper course, then takes a right angle turn to flow in a north-westerly direction. It enters the Ladakh region of Jammu and Kashmir; joins the Tsarap Chu river which later merges with the Zaskar river flowing into the Indus.

The entire catchment of the Malung river has been shaped by the action of glaciers, both present and past. The valley is fairly wide and there occur terraces on either sides of the river bed. An enormous quantity of fluvio-glacial sediments are found in the valley bottom. Snow-fed streams emanating from glaciers in the side valleys contribute their water to the Malung river.

The terrain through which this river flows in bleak and remote. It lies between the Zaskar range in the north-west and the main or great Himalaya in the south-east. This is a rain-deficient area. Vegetation is virtually absent. The Malung catchment is visited by graziers from time to time. Its middle course lies across the road from Bara La Cha pass to Leh.

MANAS RIVER

The river Manas is an important eastern Himalayan tributary of the Brahmaputra river. The main stream of this river rises in southern Tibet. It flows towards south and cuts across the main Himalayan range to enter Arunchal Pradesh near Bum La pass in the extreme north-western corner of the state. It continues to flow towards south

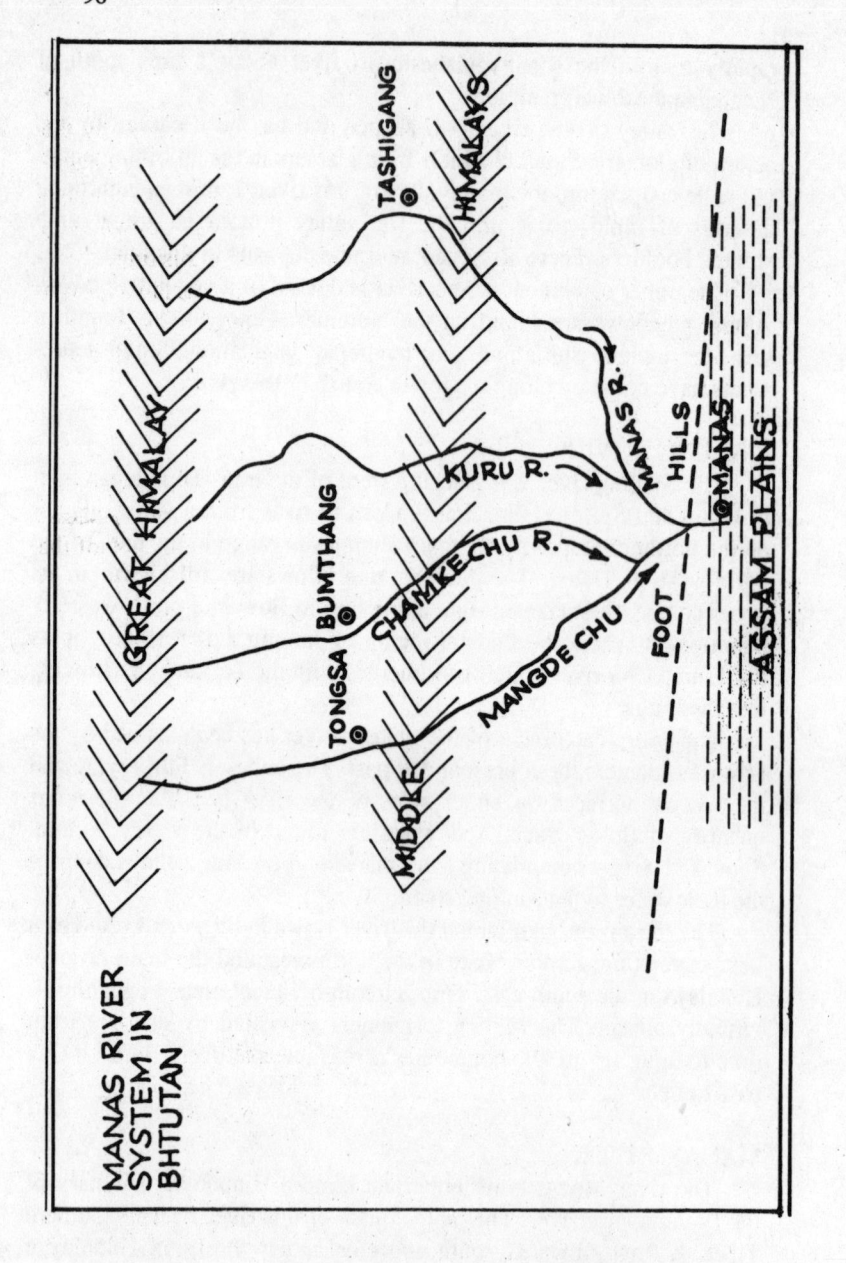

MANAS RIVER SYSTEM IN BHTUTAN

and change its course towards south-west on entering Bhutan.

Thereafter the Manas river flows in Bhutan between two offshoot ranges of the lower Himalaya in a south-westerly direction. It leaves Bhutan and enters Assam in the south-central foothills and finally drains into the Brahmaputra river opposite Goalpara.

The upper and middle courses of the Manas river flow through a deep V-shaped valley in Arunachal Pradesh and Bhutan. The valley is open in the foothills and swamps and marshes have developed along the river as it cuts across the lower hills and enters the plains.

Many snow-fed tributary rivers join the river Manas. These are--
-- the river Tawang rises near Tse La in Arunachal Pradesh and joins the Manas near the Bhutan-Arunachal border
-- the river Kurd rises in the snows of the main Himalayan range and flows towards south before merging with the Manas river
-- the river Mangde Chu drains central Bhutan. It flows in a SE direction before merging with the Manas just before the latter enters the plains.

The upper catchment of this river is covered by a perpetual cover of snow. Forests occur in the middle and lower valleys of the Manas river. The human settlements that have come up along the river Manas are Bum Gang and Tashi Gang Dzong.

MANDAKINI RIVER

The Mandakini river is an important tributary of the Alaknanda river. It drains the famous Kedarnath valley of Garhwal. It rises as two channels in the area to the east of Kedarnath. One channel drains away from the Bhagirathi Kharak glacier while the other emanates from the Satopanth glacier. These two channels merge after a short distance and form the Mandakini river.

Thereafter the river descends over a steep to gentle gradient towards south to empty itself into the Alaknanda river at Rudraparyag. The Mandakini river flows along a V-shaped valley. Huge river terraces have been formed at a number of places, viz Agustmuni and Tilwara.

The main tributaries of the Mandakini river are--
-- the river Kakra Gad drains into the Mandakini upstream of Chandrapuri
-- the river Chandrapuri Gad joins the Mandakini at the mountain hamlet of Chandrapuri
-- the river Lastar Gad merges with the Mandakini river at Tiwara.

The entire catchment of this river bears alpine, sub-alpine, temperate and sub-tropical forests. The human settlements that have come up along this river are Gauri Kund, Chandrapuri, Agustmuni and Tilwara.

MANGDE CHU RIVER

The Mangde Chu river is a tributary of the Manas river. Its source is a glacier tenanted on the southern slopes of the main Himalayan range. Three channels merge to form the mainstream of the Mangde Chu river. It then flows along a SSE course to Tongsa before turning towards SW and joining with the Manas river a short distance upstream of where the latter enters Indian territory near Manas.

A perpetual blanket of snow covers the upper catchment of this river. The valley bottom has a gentle slope which abruptly merges with the almost precipitous side slopes. Hanging valleys pour snow-melt waters into the main channel of this river from both flanks.

The middle and lower valley of the Mangde Chu river is V-shaped. River terraces occur at different levels indicating the positions at which this river once flowed. The Bumthang Chu is an important tributary of this river. It drains the eastern flank of the Mangde Chu catchment.

Alpine meadows occur on the moraines along this river. Sub-alpine, temperate and semi-evergreen forests are found at lower elevations. Terraces in the lower tract are under cultivation. Tongsa and Shemgang are two towns that have come up along this river.

MANUNI RIVER

The Manuni river is a foothill tributary of the river Beas. It rises on the southern slopes of the Dhauladhar range. Thereafter this river flows in a general direction towards south and flows into the Beas.

Steep slopes form the upper catchment of the Manuni river. There is a sharp fall in its gradient. It becomes gentler once the river enters the valley bottom of the Kangra valley.

The Manuni river meanders across the valley. There occur huge deposits of unsorted sediments and boulders along the river bed. It descends over a series of small rapids in its upper course.

Huge river terraces have formed along the Manuni river. These occur on both sides of the river bed. The terraces are under cultivation. Forests are found only in the upper catchment of this river. Riverine vegetation has come up along the river bed and on the river islands. A number of rain-fed tributaries join the Manuni river at various places.

MAO RIVER

The Mao rivers drains the central tract of southern Bhutan. It rises from the south-facing slopes of the lower Himalaya as a spring emanating from the reservoir of underground water. The Mao river than flows in a general direction towards south and enters the plains near Geylephug.

This river has carved a V-shaped valley. The prominent geomorphic features of its catchment are incised meanders, rock benches, paired and unpaired terraces, cliffs and spurs. Steep to precipitous slopes extend right upto the river bed which in turn is covered with huge boulders.

A number of small rain-fed tributaries join the Mao river. It has cut a deep gorge across the foothills before debouching into the plains. Semi-evergreen forests are found in the catchment of the Mao river. Human settlements have come up along its course.

MARDI KHOLA RIVER

This is a small snow-fed tributary of the Seti Khola river in central Nepal. The Seti Khola in turn flows into the Gandak river. It rises from the snowy wastes on the slopes of the Machhapuchhare peak and flows along a very steep gradient to merge with the Seti Khola river in the Pokhra valley.

Alpine, sub-alpine and temperate vegetation is found in the catchment of this river. Population is very sparse except along its lower course in the flat Pokhra valley.

MARKANDA RIVER

This is a small river of the Siwalik hills of the Nahan area of the Himachal Pradesh. It rises from the southern face of the lower Himalaya on the western extremity of the Kiarda dun (Paonta) valley. The Markanda is a mere trickle at its origin. Thereafter it flows along the valley bottom in a general direction towards west, turns towards south-west and emerges out of the Siwalik hills to enter the plains of Haryana.

The lower Himalayan hills of Nahan occur on the right flank of the Markanda valley while the low rolling Siwalik hills are on its left flank. The slopes vary from gentle to steep and precipitous in the upper tracts.

The discharge of this river is very low during the summer months. It increases abruptly in the monsoon season to begin to subside in autumn. The river bed is wide and dry with the water channel being confined to a narrow tract. Its bed is strewn with boulders.

Large river terraces occur along this river. These are under cultivation. Sal forests cover the hill slopes on both sides of the valley. Khair and shisham forests are found on the dry river bed.

MARKANDA (MADHYAMAHESHWARI) RIVER

The Markanda river is a tributary of the Madhyamaheshwari river in the Kedarnath valley of Garhwal. It rises from a glacier situated in a cirque on the slopes of the Madan Parbat peak. Thereafter it flows down to merge with the main river at Bantoli.

Erosion caused by glacial movement has shaped the upper valley of this river. The sides have been abraded into a U-shape. Moraines occur on the sides of the valley bottom. In its middle and lower courses the Markanda river flows along a deep V-shaped valley and steep gorge. It descends rapidly over a series of rapids in its upper reaches.

Paired and unpaired river terraces formed by this river over the past thousands of years are one of the most important geomorphic features of the Markanda valley. Others include interlocking spurs, razor-sharp ridges, steep cliffs and rock benches.

Alpine, sub-alpine and temperate forests are found in this tract. Small villages have come up along the middle and lower courses of the Markanda river.

MARSYANDI RIVER

The Marsyandi river is a tributary of the Kali Gandaki or Krishna Gandaki river in central Nepal. A large part of the basin of this river lies to the north of the main Himalayan axis. This river has a number of snow-fed tributaries. These are--

-- the Seti Khola river is a major tributary of the Marsyandi river. It drains the Pokhra valley
-- the Chapa Khola river drains the area to the north of Gorkha town
-- the Darondia Khola is another snow-fed tributary of the Marsyandi river.
-- the Trisuli river too flows into the Marsyandi river before

joining the Gandak system.

The Marsyandi river flows along a narrow V-shaped valley. It has cut a gorge across the lower Himalaya or Mahabharat Lekh. River terraces occur at different levels and these are indicative of the position at which this river once flowed.

Temperate and sub-tropical forests occur in this tract. A number of human settlements have come up along the Marsyandi river though its upper catchment is a remote and extremely cold tract.

MIRI RIVER

This is a small tributary of the Subansiri river in Arunachal Pradesh. It flows towards east from the Miri hills and joins the Subansiri downstream of Hachi.

MIRIST KHOLA RIVER

The Mirist Khola river is a tributary of the Krishna Gandaki or Gandak river in central Nepal. It originates from the snowy wastes on the south-facing slope of the Annapurna massif on the main Himalayan range. It collects snow-melt waters from a glacial amphitheatre. Small glaciers are located between the spurs in this trough. The minor channels combine to form the mainstream of the Mirist Khola.

This river flows in a general direction towards south, past interlocking spurs of the lower hills of the main Himalaya to join the Gandak or Kali Gandaki river below Dana.

The catchment of this river bears rich and dense forests. Small villages have come up along the Mirist Khola river.

MO CHU RIVER

Another name of the upper course of the Sankosh river. (For detailed description see 'Sankosh river').

MODI KHOLA RIVER

The Modi Khola river is a small tributary of the Seti Khola which in turn flows into the Marsyandi river in central Nepal. It rises from the glaciers on the southern slopes of the Annapurna massif between the Annapurna I and Machhapuchhare peak on the main Himalayan range.

Thereafter this river flows along a steep gradient to merge with the Seti Khola river which then flows into the Marsyandi river. The valley of this river is U-shaped. There occur moraines along the river bed. The water flows over a series of small waterfalls and rapids. Huge boulders are strewn all over the valley bottom.

Alpine meadows and sub-alpine and temperate forests are found in the catchment of the river. It is very sparsely populated.

MUNAWARWALI RIVER

This river is a short tributary of the Chenab river. It merges with the main river in the Munawarwali dun valley in the foothills of Jammu area.

MUTZGAH RIVER

This river is also known as the Shaksgam river. (For detailed description see 'Shaksgam river').

NANDAKINI RIVER

The river Nandakini is a tributary of the Alaknanda. It is a snow-fed river that rises from the snowy wastes at the base of the Trisul massif in the main Himalayan range along the border of Garhwal and Kumaun. Thereafter it flows in a general direction towards south-west and joins the river Alaknanda at Nandparyag.

Two main feeder streams rise from the snows at a distance of about 15 kms from each other. They merge after a short distance to form the Nandakini river. A number of other tributaries emanating from groundwater-fed springs join the Nandakini river at various places along its course.

Steep slopes occur in the upper catchment of this river. The valley is deep, V-shaped. The Nandakini has cut deep gorges in certain sections. Prominent geomorphic features of the Nandakini valley include river-cut and river-built terraces, gorges, interlocking spurs and rock benches.

Alpine, sub-alpine, temperate and sub-tropical forests are found in the Nandakini catchment. The forests of the lower catchment are degraded. Many small human settlements have come up along the Nandakini river.

NANDHAUR RIVER

The Nandhaur river is a small river draining the Siwalik hills of Uttar Pradesh. Small springs rise from the lower Himalaya and merge to form the Nandhaur river. Thereafter it flows towards south and has cut a gorge across the Siwalik hills before entering the Ganga plain.

The slopes in the upper catchment of this river are very steep. They are covered with sub-tropical forests. The gradient of the middle and lower course of this river is gentle. Riverine forests are found in this tract.

The Nandhaur river has deposited huge boulders on its bed and on the adjoining terraces. It is in spate during the rainy season. There is a marked drop in its discharge during summer.

NAYAR RIVER

The Nayar is the most important river draining the Kotdwara-Satpuli area of Garhwal. It is primarily a spring-fed river that rises from the southern slopes of the Pauri ridge. Thereafter this river flows in a general direction towards south and enters the Ganga plain after cutting a deep gorge across the Siwalik hills.

Steep slopes are a characteristic feature of the upper catchment of this river. A number of tributaries join the mainstream of the Nayar river at various places all along its course.

The principal geomorphic features that have been formed by this river are incised meanders, deep gorges, V-shaped valleys, river-cut and river-built terraces and rock benches. Broad river terraces have formed at the confluence of the Nayar river with its numerous tributaries.

Temperate forests occur in the upper catchment of this river. These give way to sub-tropical and riverine vegetation at lower elevations. The terraces occurring along this river are under cultivation. A number of human settlements have come up along this river.

NIHAL RIVER

This is a small spring-fed river that drains the Siwalik hills of Uttar Pradesh. It rises from the southern slopes of the lower Himalaya and flows in a general direction towards south. The river Nihal has cut a deep gorge across the Siwalik hills before entering the plains of western Uttar Pradesh.

This river is often in spate during the rainy season as the unprotected uplands are unable to absorb the rain water that pours down from the skies within a short span of time.

Sub-tropical and riverine forests occur in the catchment of this river. The terraces are cultivated. Boulders of various sizes have been laid down by this river over a wide zone all along its bed.

NIYAR RIVER

The Niyar river is a small glacial torrent that contributes its discharge to the Chandra-Bhaga or Chenab river in the Lahul valley of Himachal Pradesh. This river rises from a glacier on the south-facing slopes of the main or great Himalayan range. The channel flows in a south easterly direction in its upper course before taking a right angle turn and flowing towards south-west before merging with the Chenab river near the hamlet of Udaipur.

Numerous snow-fed channels flowing in from the snowy wastes tenanted in the spurs and cirques join the Niyar river all along its course. Hanging valleys pour water and ice falls into the Niyar valley.

This river descends along a very steep gradient which becomes gentler only for a short distance near its mouth once the river enters the relatively flat Chenab valley. The upper reaches of this river may freeze in winter as the entire tract remains under a thick blanket of snow for a fairly long period.

NUBRA RIVER

The river Nubra is a tributary of the Shyok river which in turn drains into the Indus river in Ladakh area of Jammu and Kashmir. This river rises from a glacier in a depression to the east of Saltoro Kangri peak and north-west of the Sasser La pass. It flows towards south-east to join the river Shyok downstream of Shyok village at the base of the Ladakh range.

The entire Nubra valley has been carved by ancient glaciers which have now receded. The valley bottom lies at an average elevation of over 4000 metres. The river descends along a steep gradient to merge with the Shyok river.

Deposits brought down by the glacier in the past ages are found strewn all over the Nubra valley. These are intermixed with fluvial deposits laid down by the running water in the recent past. Waterfalls descending from hanging valleys open into the Nubra valley at various places. Recently formed small terraces occur along the river.

The entire catchment is devoid of any type of vegetation. This is due to the high elevation and lack of rainfall. Human habitation is virtually absent in the Nubra valley.

NYAMJANG RIVER

The Nyamjang river drains the extreme part of north-north-western Arunachal Pradesh. It rises from a glacier in southern Tibet.

Thereafter this river flows in a general direction towards south, enters India through a deep gorge and merges with the Tawang river near the Bhutan-Arunachal Pradesh border.

A number of snow-fed tributaries flow into the Nyamjang river. The largest such channel drains the western part of the Nyamjang catchment and flows into the mainstream to the south-east of Shakti.

This river flows along a deep V-shaped valley. Its middle and lower catchments are densely forested. Small villages have come up along the river.

NYERA AMA RIVER

The Nyera Ama is a river of the eastern part of Bhutan. It rises from the snows on the southern face of the main Himalaya, flows across eastern Bhutan in a general direction towards south before entering the plains of Assam through the Siwalik hills.

Small channels emanating from perpetual deposits of ice in the uplands join to form the main channel of the Nyera Ama river. The upper catchment is under a cover of snow. There occur deposits of glacial sediments on either sides of this river.

The Nyera Ama river has formed terraces on the side slopes of its valley. These are at different levels indicating the position at which this river once flowed. Other geomorphic features of the Nyera Ama valley include cliffs, rock benches and interlocking spurs. This river has carved gorges across the lower and outer Himalaya.

The moraines are covered with alpine grasslands and scrub. Fir, blue pine, chir pine and oak forests are found at different elevations in the Nyera Ama valley. Many human settlements have come up along the middle and lower courses of this river.

The vegetation of this tract has been adversely affected by shifting cultivation in the past. They are in various stages of degradation.

PABAR RIVER

The Pabar river is a tributary of the Tons river which in turn drains into the river Yamuna. This river rises from the south-facing slopes of the Dhauladhar range near the border of Uttar Pradesh and Himachal Pradesh in the extreme north-eastern corner of Shimla district. The main stream is fed by the Chandra Nahan glacier and springs emanating from underground waters.

Thereafter this river flows towards SW in its upper course. It takes a U-turn and flows in a south-easterly direction in its middle and lower courses to join the Tons river at the base of the Chakrata massif near the border of Uttar Pradesh and Himachal Pradesh.

The Pabar river flows along a V-shaped valley. Many small tributaries merge with the river particularly in its upper course. The valley widens near the mouth of this river.

Sub-alpine, temperate and sub-tropical forests cover the Pabar catchment. There is a heavy biotic pressure on the forests of the lower Pabar valley. Human habitation is sparse. Settlements are found along the river Pabar particularly along its lower course which include the towns of Chirgaon, Rohru and Nerwa.

PANJANG RIVER

This river is a tributary of the Karnali river in north-western Nepal. It rises from a large glacier tenanted in the south-facing slopes of the main Himalayan range near Charkabhotgaon. Thereafter the Panjang river flows parallel to Nepal-Tibet border with the Humla mountains in the north and the Jumla range in the south. It turns towards west and flows into the Karnali river as the latter comes out of the Humla gorge.

The upper catchment of this river is glaciated. Valley glaciers open into the main glacial trough of the Panjang. The valley becomes narrower as the river flows past interlocking spurs in its middle and lower course. A number of large snow-fed tributaries join this river at various places along its courses.

Both dry and moist alpine scrub is found in the upper catchment of this river. Temperate conifer and broad-leaved forests cover the slopes at lower elevations. The Panjang valley is inhabited by semi-nomadic communities. Charkabhotgaon and Phijorgaon are two villages of this tract.

PARBATI RIVER

The river Parbati is a tributary of the river Beas. It rises in the snowy wastes upstream of Manikaran on the foothills of the main Himalayan range in Kulu district of Himachal Pradesh. The glacier which feeds this river descends down from the steep southern slopes of the main Himalaya. The Parbati river rises as small channels flowing away from the tongue of this glacier. Thereafter they merge and begin to flow towards west to join the river Beas at Shamshi in the Kulu valley.

The valley of the Parbati river is deep and narrow right from its origin to its confluence with the Beas. Small terraces are found on either sides of the river. These have been formed by it over the past thousands of years. A number of small streams merge with the Parbati. Hot water springs at Manikaran pour their water into this river.

The entire catchment of the Parbati river is covered by sub-alpine temperate and sub-tropical coniferous and deciduous forests. The important human settlements that have come up along this river are Manikaran and Kasol.

PARE RIVER

This is a small tributary of the Tsarap Chu river which in turn drains into the Zaskar river in Ladakh. The Pare river rises from the snowy wastes of a glacier on the south-facing slopes of the Zaskar range. Thereafter it flows for a short distance towards south-east in its upper course, turns towards south-west and merges with the Tsarap Chu river near Sutak.

A permanent cover of snow clothes the upper catchment of this river. A number of small snow-fed streams drain into the main river at various places. The valley is U-shaped with steep side slopes.

This tract is deficient in rain as it lies across the main or great Himalaya. Vegetation is sparse. The road from Bara La Cha pass to Leh crosses the Pare valley.

PARLA RIVER

A small tributary of the Dhauliganga river in Garhwal. It rises from the Parla cirque and drains small channels from hanging valleys. The river drains into the Dhauliganga river at the Geldung camping ground.

PARO RIVER

This river is also known as the Paro Chu. It is a tributary of the Raidak river in west-central Bhutan. The Paro river rises from a glacier to the north of the old fort of Dukve dzong on the southern slopes of the main Himalaya. Thereafter it flows in a general direction towards south-south-east and merges with the Raidak river at Confluence.

The upper tracts of the Paro catchment are under a perpetual cover of snow. Alpine meadows are found on the moraines that occur along the upper course of this river. Sub-alpine and temperate forests are found along its middle and lower courses. The terraces around

Paro and downstream of it are under cultivation. Amongst the main human settlements that have come up along this river are Dukve dzong and Paro. The town of Confluence lies at the confluence of the Paro with the Raidak river.

PATLIKHUL RIVER

The Patlikhul river is a tributary of the Beas river in Manali area of Himachal Pradesh. It rises from the snows on the southern slopes of the Pir Panjal range. Thereafter it flows into the Beas river upstream of Kulu.

PATSARI RIVER

The Patsari river is a small spring-fed tributary of the Pabar river which in turn is a feeder of the Tons river. This river rises as a spring emanating from the reservoir of underground water in the lower Himalayan hills near Kharapatthar in Shimla district of Himachal Pradesh.

Thereafter this river flows along a steep gradient in a general direction towards north-east to join the Pabar river near the mountain hamlet of Patsari about 10 kms downstream of Rohru.

The main geomorphic features of this tract include interlocking spurs, V-shaped valley and terraces formed by the deposits laid down by the river in the past. Its bed is strewn with boulders of various sizes.

Fir, spruce, blue pine, deodar, oak and chir pine forests occur in the catchment of this river. Small villages have come up along its course.

PHOKSUMDO RIVER

The Phoksumdo river is a tributary of the Bheri river in north-central Nepal. It rises from the Phoksumdo glacier. The entire catchment of this river has been carved by the action of glaciers.

PINDAR RIVER

The river Pindar is an important tributary of the river Alaknanda. It rises from the Pindari glacier lying at the base of the Nanda Kot massif on the Alaknanda-Kali water-divide in Garhwal. Thereafter this river flows towards south in its upper course and then gradually turns towards west to merge with the Alaknanda river at Karanparyag in Chamoli district.

The upper catchment of this river comprises of steep snowclad slopes that descend from towering heights right upto the water channel. Moraines are commonly found in this tract. Deep V-shaped valleys and gorges have been formed by this river in its middle and lower courses. The entire river bed is strewn with gigantic boulders brought down by the Pindar river during the past thousands of years.

A number of small snow-fed tributaries join the Pindar river at different places. The most prominent amongst these are the river Rishi ganga draining the snows at the base of the Nanda Devi massif.

The entire catchment (except areas above the snow line) is covered by good forests. These include alpine meadows, sub-alpine, temperate and sub-tropical coniferous and broad-leaved forests. Small human settlements exist all along the middle and lower courses of the Pindar river.

POONCH RIVER

The river Poonch drains the Poonch area of the foothills of Jammu and Kashmir. It is a tributary of the river Jhelum. This river rises from the south-facing slopes of the Pir Panjal range in the south-western part of the state. It then flows towards south for a short distance, makes a U-turn, flows in a westerly direction and finally attains a south-westerly course to merge with the Jhelum near Mirpur.

The steep slopes of the Pir Panjal range form the upper catchment of this river. It is a small gurgling water channel in this tract and descends along a very steep gradient till it reaches the foothills. The channel widens as more and more tributaries open into the mainstream. The valley too opens up and the Poonch river begins to flow at a leisurely pace in its middle and lower course.

Large river terraces have formed along the river downstream of Poonch town. These are under cultivation. The upper catchment is covered by dense forests while the vegetation of the middle and lower catchments is under an intense biotic pressure. Many human settlements have come up along the river Poonch. These include the towns of Poonch, Kotli and Mirpur.

PUSHPAWATI RIVER

The river Pushpawati drains the famous Valley of Flowers in Garhwal. This river rises from the east Kamet glacier lying at the base of the main Himalayan mountain wall near the central part of the border of Garhwal with Tibet. Thereafter it flows in a general direction towards south to merge with another mainstream of the Dhauliganga near Ghagharia. The channel is known as the Dhauliganga downstream of Ghagharia.

The legend says that during their years in exile the Pandavas saw flowers floating down a river. They named it Pushpawati. The upper valley of the Pushpawati river or the Valley of Flowers was brought to the attention of the outside world by the Mt. Kamet expedition of 1936. It is so named due to the virtually endless carpet of alpine flowers that cover the valley in autumn each year.

The upper valley of the Pushpawati is U-shaped. It has been carved by the action of glaciers. The river flows past thick glacial deposits. A number of smaller tributaries fed by tributary glaciers join it at various places within the valley. It has cut a deep gorge in its lower course.

The upper tracts are under a permanent cover of snow. Alpine, sub alpine and temperate vegetation occurs in the middle and lower catchments of this river. Human habitation is very sparse. Ghagharia is the last settlement before one enters the Valley of Flowers. The valley is visited by many tourists but there is no permanent settlement within the valley.

RAHUGHAT KHOLA RIVER

This river rises from the glaciers on the southern slopes of the Dhaulagiri massif. It flows towards south-west in its glacial trough, then turns towards south-east and merges with the Krishna Gandaki river above Beni in central Nepal. The Rahughat Khola river is formed by small channels of snow-melt waters originating from the snouts of glaciers and snow-fields. These channels form a network which merges to form the mainstream of this river.

Thereafter this river flows along a gentle gradient in its trough and then enters a narrow valley where its gradient becomes very steep. Moraines are found on the valley floor in the form of small humps. Fluvio-glacial sediments occur lower down the valley.

The water descends past huge boulders. It is joined by smaller snow-fed tributaries enroute. Terraces line both flanks of the Rahughat valley. They indicate the levels at which this river once flowed.

The upper tracts are under permanent cover of snow. Alpine pastures, sub-alpine, temperate and sub-tropical forests are found in the Rahughat valley. Scattered settlements have come up along this river.

RAIDAK RIVER

The Raidak river system drains western Bhutan. The main feeder tributaries of the Raidak are--
- -- the river Thi Chu rises in the snows of the main or great Himalaya north of Thimpu. Thereafter it flows towards south to form the Raidak downstream of Chukho
- -- the river Paro Chu rises in the area to the north-west of Dukve Dzong. It merges with the Thi Chu at Confluence
- -- the river Ha Chu rises in the area to the north-west of Ha. It merges with the Thi Chu flowing in from the north to form the Raidak between Chukho and Confluence.

Thereafter the river Raidak drains across the lower hills of Bhutan to enter the Brahmaputra plains. It merges with the main channel of the Brahmaputra river in northern Bangladesh.

This river flows along a V-shaped valley. It has cut across the lower Himalaya and the foothills through narrow gorges. The entire catchment is covered by forests. The human settlements that have come up along this river are Thimpu, Confluence and Chukho.

RAMGANGA RIVER

The river Ramganga drains south-western Kumaun. It is a tributary of the Ganga river. This river rises from the lower Himalayan slopes in central Kumaun on the south-eastern part of the water-divide of the Alaknanda river. It is essentially fed by springs emanating from reservoirs of underground water. Channels from a number of such springs merge to form the mainstream of this river.

Thereafter it winds its way across the lower Himalayan hills of Almora district. This river has carved a deep, V-shaped valley. Amongst the prominent geomorphic features found in this tract are incised meanders, paired and unpaired terraces, interlocking spurs, waterfalls, rock benches, cliffs and towering ridges.

The Ramganga river flows through the dun valley of Corbett national park. A dam has been erected across this river at Kalagarh. It enters the plains downstream of Kalagarh and joins the Ganga river near Kannauj in Uttar Pradesh.

Forests occur in the entire catchment of this river. The vegetation is very dense in the Corbett national park area. The main human settlements that have come up along this river are Ganai and Dhikala.

RAIDAK RIVER SYSTEM IN BHUTAN

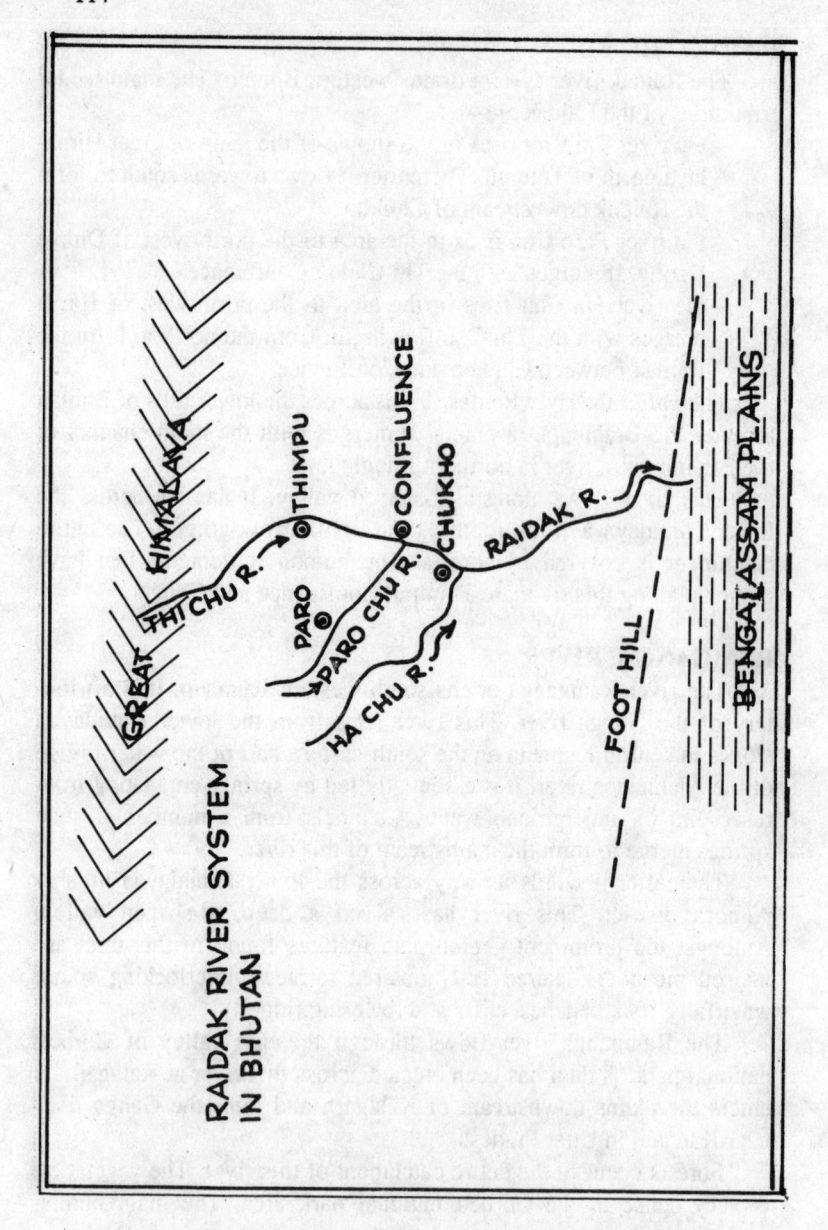

RAMGANGA (SARJU) RIVER

This river is a tributary of the Sarju river which in turn flows into the Kali river in Kumaun. It rises from a small glacier on the south-east slopes of the water-divide between Garhwal and Kumaun. The Ramganga (Sarju) river then flows in a general direction towards south-east before flowing into the Sarju river, a short distance upstream of the mountain hamlet of Pancheshwar.

The upper catchment of this river has been shaped by the action of glaciers. Moraines occur on the valley bottom. These have been deposited by past glacial activity. The valley becomes narrower once the river enters its middle course as this tract has almost entirely been carved by running water. The river bed is strewn with boulders of various sizes. River terraces occur all along its course.

The Ramganga (Sarju) river has carved a V-shaped valley in its middle and lower courses. Alpine, sub-alpine, temperate and sub-tropical forests are found in this tract. Many small human settlements have come up along the Ramganga (Sarju) river.

RANGIT RIVER

The river Rangit is a tributary of the Teesta river. It rises from a glacier on the south-eastern slopes of the Kanchenjunga massif in Sikkim. Thereafter it flows towards west to merge with the Teesta river at Mangan.

The upper catchment of this river has been carved by the action of glaciers. Gigantic mountain walls rim the north-western boundary of the upper Rangit valley. Hanging valleys open into the main valley at several points.

The middle and lower courses of this river flow along valleys carved by the action of running water. Small terraces have been laid down by the river over the past thousands of years. The valley widens near the confluence of this river with the Teesta river.

The upper tracts are under a perpetual cover of snow. Alpine pastures occur near the snowline. Sub-alpine and temperate forests are found at lower elevations. Human habitation is very sparse.

RAPTI RIVER

The Rapti river is an important tributary of the Ghagra system. It drains south-central Nepal. The mainstream of this river rises as a spring on the southern slopes of the lower Himalaya in the area to the north of Pyuthan. This river is essentially fed by underground water and rain. It flows towards south in its upper course, then attains a westerly course through the famous Rapti dun valley before turning towards south-east near Nepalganj and entering the plains of India where this river flows into the Ghagra.

Small tributaries rising from the lower Himalaya and Siwalik hills which join the Rapti river at various places are--
-- a tributary rises from the Mahabharat Lekh to the north-east of Salyan and flows towards south-east to join the Rapti downstream of Pyuthan
-- small tributaries rise in the area to the west of Tansen, flow towards south and merge with the Rapti in the plains of India.

The Rapti river flows for a considerable distance in a dun valley lying between the lower Himalaya in the north and the Siwalik hills in the south. This is known as the Rapti dun valley. It has cut a gorge across the Siwalik hills to the east of Nepalganj.

The entire catchment of the Rapti river is covered with subtropical oak, pine and sal forests. Riverine vegetation has come up along the river. Amongst the towns along this river are Libangaon and Pyuthan.

RAVI RIVER

The river Ravi is one of the five major tributaries of river Indus. It rises in the Bara Banghal area of Himachal Pradesh in the tract bounded by the Pir Panjal range in the north and the Dhauladhar range in the south. Two main feeder streams merge to form the Ravi--
-- the Bhadal that is fed by a glacier on the southern slopes of the Pir Panjal
-- the Tant Gari which too originates from the snows on the southern slopes of the Pir Panjal.

Thereafter the Ravi river flows towards west along a V-shaped valley. There occur paired and unpaired terraces on either sides of the channel. It is joined near Chamba by a small river flowing in from Kistwar area of Jammu & Kashmir in the west.

In its middle course the Ravi takes a U-turn downstream of Chamba where it has cut across the Dhauladhar range and begins to follow a south-westerly course. It emerges from the hills near Madhopur where a small dam has been erected across its course. The Ravi merges with the Chenab in Pakistan.

Different types of forests cover the entire catchment of the Ravi river. Important human settlements that exist along this river are

Bharmour, Chamba and Madhopur.

RIBANG RIVER

The Ribang river is a small tributary of the Tenga river which in turn drains into the Kameng system. This river drains the lower Dafla hills in east-central Arunachal Pradesh.

Two streams fed by underground water merge to form the Ribang river. The main channel flows in a general direction towards south and merges with the Tenga river east of Karangania.

RIKHI GAD RIVER

This is a small tributary of the Dudhganga river in Garhwal. It drains into the main channel in the upper course.

RISHIGANGA RIVER

The Rishiganga river is a tributary of the Pindar river in Garhwal. It drains the snows at the base of the Nanda Devi massif.

RISPANA RIVER

This river drains the central part of Dehradun valley in Garhwal. It is a tributary of the river Song. The Rispana river rises as a small spring at the base of the Mussoorie ridge near Rajpur. Thereafter it flows along a south-westerly course and passes along the eastern outskirts of Dehradun town before draining into the river Song.

The reservoir of underground water in the towering Mussoorie ridge feeds this river all round the year though there is a considerable drop in its discharge during the hot summer months. A number of small springs join this river in the Rajpur area. The east canal which passes through Dehradun city has been diverted away from the Rispana river.

Huge terraces formed by the thick pile of sediments brought down by the Rispana occur all along the river. The river bed too is almost entirely covered by boulders of various sizes. The river channel is confined to a small part of the river bed.

The Rispana river forms the eastern boundary of Dehradun city. A number of colonies have now come up to the east of this river. The land along the river is either a part of the city or is under cultivation.

RUPIN RIVER

The river Rupin is one of the two mainstreams which form the

Tons river at the border of Himachal Pradesh and Garhwal. It rises from a glacier near Rupin pass at the base of the main Himalayan slopes of Kinnaur. Thereafter the Rupin river flows in a south easterly course through the remote Dodra-Kawar area of Shimla district, enters Garhwal and joins the Supin at Naitwar to form the Tons river.

The upper tracts of the Rupin catchment are glaciated. There occur hanging valleys, waterfalls, terminal and lateral moraines. Snow-melt waters from side valleys containing glaciers drain into the Rupin river at various places.

The river has cut a deep, V-shaped gorge in its middle and lower course. There occur river terraces on both the side slopes. Other geomorphic features include incised meanders and rock benches.

The valley of the Rupin river is very remote. It can be approached from Rohru in Himachal Pradesh after crossing the Chansel pass. Alpine, sub-alpine and temperate conifer and broad-leaved forests occur in the Rupin catchment. Dodra and Kawar are two large villages situated on high terraces on either sides of the Rupin river.

SAJE RIVER

This is the headwaters of the Siyom river which in turn drains into the Dihang or Siang or Brahmaputra river. The Saje river drains the south-western slopes of the Bokar hills. It rises from a glacier and flows south-westwards to join the Siyom river upstream of Gasheng village. Dense forests are found in the catchment of the Saje river.

SAINJ RIVER

The river Sainj is a tributary of the Beas river. It rises from the water-divide of the Beas and Satluj rivers in the lower ranges of the main Himalaya to the east of Kulu in Himachal Pradesh. Thereafter the river flows towards south-west to join the Beas just before it cuts across the Dhauladhar range near Larji.

A number of tributaries join the Sainj river both from the northern and southern flanks of its valley. The Sainj valley is V-shaped and the river flows past a series of interlocking spurs. It has widened near the mouth of the river.

Dense temperate and sub-tropical forests are found in the Sainj valley. A number of human settlements have come up along the Sainj river.

SALTORO RIVER

The river Saltoro is a tributary of the Hughe river which in turn drains into the Shyok. It rises as two mainstreams from glaciers at the base of the Saltoro Kangri peak in Ladakh. The north-western mainstream flows towards SE and then turns towards SW to merge with the north-eastern mainstream flowing towards north-west.

The two mainstreams join together in the middle course of the river and the Saltoro flows for a short distance before draining into the Hushe river.

The entire valley of the river Saltoro has been carved by the action of glaciers. Deposits of moraines brought down by ancient glaciers are found all along the river right from its origin to the mouth. Small tributary snow-fed streams empty themselves into the main river, usually from hanging valleys at different places.

The discharge of this river increases in late summer when the snow on the high mountains melts at a very fast rate. The entire catchment is devoid of a vegetative cover. Human habitation is virtually absent and the tract is bleak and desolate.

SANKOSH RIVER

This is a major river which drains west-central Bhutan. It rises as Mo Chu river from the snowy wastes at the base of the main Himalayan range of northern Bhutan. Thereafter it flows in a general direction towards south to enter the plains west of Sarbhang.

The upper catchment of the Sankosh river is glaciated. The high mountain tops are under a permanent cover of snow. The middle and lower courses flow along V-shaped valleys that have been carved by running water. The main geomorphic features of this tract include river terraces, interlocking spurs, cliffs and ridges. It has cut deep gorges across the lower Himalaya and the outer foothills.

A number of large snow-fed streams join the Sankosh river at Punakha and Wangdu Phodrang. Spring-fed streams merge with the main river in its middle and lower courses.

The entire catchment of the Sankosh river is covered by forests. These range from alpine meadows in the upper tracts to sub-tropical forests at lower elevations. The main human settlements that have come up along this river are Gasa Dzong, Punakha, Wangdu Phodrang and Chirang.

This river finally merges with the main channel of the Brahmaputra near the Indo-Bangladesh border.

SAPT KOSI RIVER

Another name of the Kosi river that drains Nepal. (For detailed description see 'Kosi river system').

SARJU RIVER

The river Sarju is the largest tributary of the Kali river. It rises in the area to the north-west of Baijnath in central Kumaun. The Sarju river flows towards south in its upper course, then turns towards south-east and joins the Kali river at Pancheshwar.

The Sarju river and its network of tributaries are fed by springs emanating from reservoirs of underground water. The entire valley of the Sarju has been shaped by the action of running water. The prominent geomorphic features include incised meanders, terraces and rock benches.

The Ramganga (Sarju) river is an important tributary of the Sarju. It flows in from the north and joins the Sarju river in its lower course to the north-west to Pancheshwar.

This river flows along the northern base of the Almora massif. The entire catchment is covered by temperate and sub-tropical forests which are under a severe biotic pressure due to the high population density in this tract. A number of human settlements have come up along the Sarju river. The temple town of Baijnath and Pancheshwar are the most important amongst them.

SATLUJ RIVER

The river Satluj is the most important of the five major tributaries of the Indus system. It rises as Langchhen Khabab river from Rakas lake near the holy Mansarovar lake in Tibet. It flows for a considerable distance before entering Himachal Pradesh near Shipki La.

The Satluj river flows along a south-western course in Himachal. The river has carved spectacular gorges where it has cut across the Zaskar, main Himalaya and Dhauladhar ranges. It flows at the base of the Shimla ridge and enters the lower hills in Bilaspur area where the gigantic Bhakra dam has been erected across it. The Satluj river then enters the plains of Punjab to finally drain into the Indus in Pakistan.

Important tributaries of the Satluj in Himachal Pradesh are--
-- the river Spiti rises in the northern slopes of the main Himalayan range. It drains into the Satluj river at Namgia
-- the Baspa river rises from the snows along the northern U.P.-H.P. border. It flows into the Satluj upstream of Kalpa.

The upper tracts of the Satluj valley are under a permanent cover of snow. Alpine, sub-alpine, temperate and sub-tropical forests are found at different elevations. Many human settlements have come up along the Satluj river. The important amongst these are Namgia, Kalpa, Rampur and Bilaspur.

SETI RIVER

The Seti river is an important western tributary of the Ghagra river system that drains western Nepal. It rises from the snow-fields and glaciers around the twin peaks of Api and Nampa on the south facing slopes of the main Himalaya near the border of Kumaun-Nepal and Tibet. It flows towards south-east, attains a south-westerly direction before turning towards south-east once again and flowing into the Karnali river. The Seti catchment marks the water-divide between the Kali river system in the west and the Gandak river system in the east.

The Seti river has cut a spectacular gorge across the lower Himalaya or Mahabharat Lekh. Its valley is V-shaped. Broad river terraces occur along the lower course of this river. Small terraces have been formed in the upper reaches.

The northern part of the Seti catchment consists of snowy wastes and glaciers. Alpine meadows are found on moraines. Temperate forests occur lower down the valley while sub-tropical forests cover the slopes south of the Mahabharat Lekh. These are under heavy biotic pressure. The largest town along this river is Silgarhi. It lies on the route from Pokhra to Pithoragarh (Kumaun).

SETI KHOLA RIVER

The Seti Khola river is an important tributary of the Gandak or Krishna Gandaki river in central Nepal. It rises from a glacier and adjoining snow-fields on the slopes of Annapurna III peak. It flows in a general direction towards south-east before joining the Marsyandi river which leads to the Krishna Gandaki river.

This river drains the famous Pokhra valley. It is believed that the upliftment of the Mahabharat Lekh blocked this river and led to the formation of the lakes in this valley. The Seti Khola river has cut a gorge across the Mahabharat Lekh.

A number of tributaries join the Seti Khola river. These are--
-- the Modi Khola rises from the Annapurna Himal and flows into the Seti Khola river.
-- the Mardi Khola river rises from the Machhapuchhare peak and

joins the Seti Khola in the Pokhra valley.

This river has developed large terraces particularly in the Pokhra valley. It flows though limestone deposits for a short distance and appears to be lost amongst the caves and tunnels.

Further downstream the Seti Khola river has cut a fantastic gorge across the Mahabharat Lekh. It then pours its water into the Marsyandi or Gandak.

Rich forests occur in the upper catchment of this river. These have been cleared for cultivation in the Pokhra valley. Pokhra is the largest town that has come up along the Seti Khola river.

SHAKSGAM RIVER

This river drains the extreme northern part of Ladakh, lying to the north of the Karakoram range. The Shaksgam river is also known as the Mutzgam river. It rises as two channels from the north-western flank of the famous Siachen glacier. Thereafter these two streams merge to form the main river. It flows in a north-westerly direction.

The valley of the Shaksgam river is flanked in the left by the towering Karakoram range and on the right by the Aghil range which forms the boundary of Ladakh and Tibet. It takes a U-turn and has cut a deep gorge across the Aghil range before leaving Indian territory. This river flows into the Yarkan river in Tibet.

The entire valley of this glacier has been carved by the action of glaciers. The side slopes house small glaciers which pour their water into the mainstream. The number of such hanging valleys is more on the left flank of the Shaksgam valley.

The valley bottom is littered with vast glacial deposits. These are both in the form of lateral and terminal moraines. A part of this river freezes for long periods in winter. There is an abrupt increase in its discharge during the late summer months.

The tract in which this river flows is a cold desert. Vegetative growth is virtually absent. This valley is occasionally visited by travellers.

SHERI RIVER

The Sheri river is a small tributary of the Manas river in eastern Bhutan. It rises from the lower hills of the main Himalayan range, flows in a general direction towards south to merge with the mainstream of the Manas.

This river flows along a deep V-shaped valley. It has cut a gorge across the lower Himalaya. The main geomorphic features of the Sheri catchment are incised meanders and river-cut and river-built terraces.

Bulk of its catchment is covered with thick blue pine, chir, pine fir and deciduous forests. Agriculture is restricted to only a small proportion of the total land area of this catchment.

SHIGAR RIVER

The Shigar river is a small right bank tributary of the Indus river in its course through Ladakh. This river rises from the Hispar glacier at the base of the Haramosh and Kanjut Sar peaks in northern Ladakh. Thereafter it flows towards south-east and joins the Indus at Skardu.

An important tributary of the Shigar river rises from the Baltoro glacier at the base of the Masherbrum peak and flows towards west to join the main channel of the Shigar in its middle course. Thus the Shigar system drains the melt-waters of two of the most important glaciers of the Karakoram range.

This river descends along a very steep gradient. Its entire catchment has been influenced by the action of glaciers. The valley is deep in its upper reaches but widens near its mouth. A small river island has formed at the junction of the mainstream with the tributary draining the Baltoro glacier.

The catchment of this river is virtually devoid of a vegetative cover due to its high altitude and scarcity of rainfall. Human habitation is sparse. Skardu is the largest settlement in this tract.

SHIGAR (SOUTH) RIVER

This river is left bank tributary of the river Indus in Ladakh. It rises from the glacier at the base of the Nunkun peak on the north-facing slopes of the main Himalayan mountain wall which hems the Kashmir valley. Thereafter this river drains towards north and merges with the Indus river at Marol, upstream of Skardu.

Steep slopes are a characteristic feature of the upper catchment of this river. Other geomorphic features include hanging valleys, moraines, eskers and cirques.

A number of snow-fed tributaries join the river Shigar (south) at various places. These include--

-- the river Dras which rises from the northern slopes of the main
   Himalayan mountain wall joins the main channel at Kargil
-- the river Shiugo rising from the main Himalaya

-- the river Suru rising from the main Himalaya
-- the river Wakha rising from the main Himalaya.

Vegetation is confined to alpine meadows on sheltered moraines and stripes along snow-melt waters. Human habitation is sparse. The important settlements along this river include Kargil, Tolti and Marol.

SHIMSHAL RIVER

This is a small tributary of the river Hunza. It rises from a glacier lying at the northern base of the Kanjut Sar massif in the area to the north of the Karakoram range in the extreme north-western part of Jammu and Kashmir. Two mainstreams of this river originate in different depressions of an offshoot of the Karakoram range. They merge where the two valleys meet and flow as the mainstream of the Shimshal towards west to merge with the Hunza river upstream of Baltit.

The valley of the river Shimshal is U-shaped. Thick glacial deposits cover the valley bottom across which the channel of the Shimshal meanders. Small snow-fed tributaries join the river at various places.

There is an increase in the discharge of this river in late summer when the glacier melts at a faster pace. Flash floods may occur in mid-afternoon during this season when the water level rises abruptly.

The entire catchment of the Shimshal river is devoid of a vegetative cover. Human habitation is restricted to along the Hunza river.

SHIUGO RIVER

The Shiugo is a small tributary of Shigar (south) river system. It rises from the north-eastern slopes of the main Himalayan range near Burzil pass. Permanent deposits of snow feed this river. Thereafter the Shiugo river flows towards east and merges with the Dras river upstream of Kargil.

Glacial action has shaped the present topography of the Shiugo catchment. A snow-fed tributary from the southern slopes of the Deosai mountains meets the main river a short distance upstream of where it merges with the Dras.

Vegetation is confined to alpine meadows on moraines and along channels of snow-melt waters. Human habitation is very sparse in the Shiugo valley.

SHYOK RIVER

The Shyok river is an important tributary of the Indus river in

Ladakh. The mainstream rises from the snowy wastes on the Despang plains in northern Ladakh, north of the Karakoram range. The river flows towards west in its initial stages, then turns towards south-east and makes a U-turn near Shyok to flow towards north-west. It flows into the Indus about 40 kms upstream of Skardu.

Many tributaries join the Shyok river. Important amongst these are--
-- the Chipshap river which is the headwaters of the Shyok system
-- the Galiwan river joining the Shyok from the north-east
-- the Chus river flowing in from the south-east from Chushul area
-- the Nubra river which joins the Shyok river upstream of Siari
-- the Saltoro river that merges with the main channel near Khapalu.

This river makes a V-shaped bend around the Karakoram range and marks the south-eastern extremity of this mountain system.

The entire catchment of this river is almost devoid of a vegetative cover. The important human settlements that have come up along this river are Shukpa Kunzang, Shyok, Siari and Khapalu.

SIANG RIVER

Another name for the Brahmaputra river as it passes through Arunachal Pradesh. (For detailed description see 'Brahmaputra river' or 'Dihang river').

SIKANG RIVER

Another name of the Dihang river which drains the Mishmi hills of Arunachal Pradesh. (For detailed description see 'Dihang river').

SIND RIVER

The river Sind is a tributary of the Jhelum river. It rises from the permanent deposits of snow that occur in the depressions on the south-facing slopes of the main Himalayan range which hems the northern part of the Srinagar valley in Jammu and Kashmir.

It descends along a steep gradient from the great Himalaya and enters the Kashmir valley. Thereafter this river slowly winds its way across the valley towards south and drains into the river Jhelum near Srinagar. Its speed in this tract is very slow.

Very steep slopes occur in the upper catchment of this river. Alpine, sub-alpine and temperate forests are found in this tract. The area along this river as it flows through the valley bottom is under cultivation.

SIUL RIVER

The Siul river is a tributary of the Ravi river. It rises from the tract between the Dhauladhar and Pir Panjal ranges near the Jammu and Kashmir and Himachal Pradesh border. Thereafter this river flows towards east, takes a U-turn and attains a south-westerly course before flowing into the Ravi river downstream of Chamba.

A number of tributaries join the Siul river. The most prominent amongst these are--

-- the river Baira which rises from the south-facing slopes of the Pir Panjal range in Chamba district and merges with the Siul where the latter river makes a prominent U-turn.

The Siul river system is fed both by snow-melt waters and spring waters. Its valley is U-shaped. The main geomorphic features of this tract include interlocking spurs, terraces and ridges.

The entire catchment of this river is covered by temperate and sub-tropical forests which are in various stages of degradation due to very heavy biotic pressure. Human habitation is in the form of small settlements that have come up along the course of this river.

SIYOM RIVER

This river is a tributary of the Dihang or Siang or Brahmaputra river in Arunachal Pradesh. It rises from a glacier on the south-facing slopes of the main Himalaya in north-central part of the state. Thereafter it drains in a general direction towards south, then turns westwards and flows into the Dihang or Siang near Pangin.

A number of tributaries join the Siyom river. The Saje river is the most prominent amongst these. Amongst the villages that have come up along this river are Gasheng, Yiyu, Along and Jiningo.

SOAN RIVER

The Soan river is a foothill tributary of the Satluj river in Himachal Pradesh. It rises from the southern slopes of the Siwalik range also known locally as the Solasinghi range in the tract to the east of the Beas gap across the southern periphery of the Kangra valley.

It flows for a short distance towards south, then attains a south-easterly course to join the Satluj river near its gorge across the Siwalik hills which form the boundary of Himachal Pradesh and Punjab. Three large tributaries rising from the southern slopes of the Solasinghi hills join the Soan river in its middle and lower course.

The slopes in the Soan catchment vary from gentle to steep. Its gradient is not very steep. There occur river terraces all along this river. Boulders of various sizes have been deposited along the river bed. The discharge of this river drops down drastically in summer. However it is in spate during the monsoons.

Dry deciduous and riverine forests occur in the catchment of the Saon river. The terraces are under cultivation. Many villages have come up along the course of the Soan river.

SON BHADRA RIVER

This is a short Siwalik river that flows into the main stream of the Gandak river near the Indo-Nepalese border. It rises from the southern slopes of the lower Himalaya, thereafter it flows along a longitudinal valley and cuts through the Siwalik hills or Churia range before merging with the Gandak.

Steeply dipping sedimentary strata of the Siwalik system occur on either sides of the Son Bhadra river. The water has developed many pot holes on the river bed particularly along its lower course.

Sub-tropical forests are found in the lower catchment of this river. These have been degraded due to heavy biotic pressure. Many small human settlements have come up along the Son Bhadra river.

SONG RIVER

The Song river drains the central and eastern part of Dehradun valley. It rises as a spring-fed stream from the south-facing slopes of the Mussoorie ridge to the east of Rajpur. Underground waters feed this river and its tributaries. It flows along a south-west course in its upper reaches. Thereafter it slowly turns towards east and joins the Ganga river between Rishikesh and Hardwar.

This river is one of the largest rivers draining Dehradun valley. Steep slopes hem the northern catchment of this river. Its gradient is very steep in the upper course. However the speed of this river is greatly reduced once it enters the valley.

Boulders of various sizes have been deposited all along the bed of this river. In certain sections there occur large terraces that are under cultivation. Sal forests are found along this river downstream of Lachhiwala. The dry river bed bears khair and shisham forests.

The Song river flows past a beautiful tract in its lower reaches.

Dense forests occur on either sides of the river near its confluence with the Ganga. Amongst the settlements that have come up along this river are Lachhiwala, Kansrao and Satyanarayan.

SPITI RIVER

The river Spiti is a large tributary of the Satluj river in Himachal Pradesh. This river rises as a series of small snow-fed streams from the glaciers on the northern slopes of the main Himalayan range in Spiti area. Thereafter it winds its way across the Spiti valley in a general direction towards south-east and flows into the Satluj at Namgia soon after the latter river enters Indian territory. Waters draining the famous Pin valley area are also a part of the Spiti river system.

The valley of the Spiti river resembles the Tibetan tract which lies towards north across the international border. Its position across the main Himalayan range deprives it from the benefit of the SW monsoons which cause widespread rains in most parts of India from June to September. The mountains are barren and largely devoid of a vegetative cover. Vegetation is restricted to sheltered moraines and strips along channels formed by snow-melt waters.

Huge mountains rise to very high elevations on either sides of the Spiti river and its numerous tributaries. The valley has largely been influenced by the action of ancient glaciers. Almost barren river terraces have been deposited by the river and its tributaries. These contain a mixture of glacial and fluvial sediments. The river attains peak discharge in late summers when snow on the mountains melts. The Spiti river may freeze occasionally in winter.

The main settlements that have come up along the Spiti river and its tributaries are Hansi and Dhankar Gompa.

SUBANSIRI RIVER

The Subansiri is a major eastern Himalayan tributary of the Brahmaputra. It rises from the snows on the southern slopes of the trans-Himalayan tract of Tibet and enters Arunachal Pradesh near Longju. This river has cut a deep gorge across the main Himalayan range. This river is also called Tsari Chu river.

The Subansiri river and its tributaries drain the central tract of Arunachal Pradesh. The mainstream flows towards south in its upper and middle courses and then turns towards south-south-west to join the Brahmaputra downstream of Borduttighat.

This river flows along a V-shaped valley. The Abor hills are to its east while the Miri hills are in the east. It flows across the interlocking spurs of the lower Himalayan range near Dolungmukh. The valley is fairly wide in the foothills of Arunachal Pradesh. It enters the plains of Assam before joining the Brahmaputra. There occur large islands and sand banks in the Brahmaputra at its confluence with the Subansiri river.

Numerous tributaries join the Subansiri river. These include the following--
- the rivers Yume Chhu and Chaval Chhu which rise from the snows in southern Tibet
- the Miri river that flows towards east from the Miri hills and joins the Subansiri river downstream of Hachi
- many small tributaries join the Subansiri river near its confluence with the Brahmaputra.

Except the upper tracts, the entire catchment of this river bears dense forests. The main settlements that have come up along the Subansiri river are Longju, Dolungmukh and Borduttighat.

SUKETI RIVER

The Suketi river is a small tributary of the Beas river in the Kangra valley of Himachal Pradesh. It rises from the south facing slopes of the Dhauladhar range. The river is joined by many smaller tributaries as it winds its way across the Kangra valley to merge with the Beas.

The upper catchment of the river consists of steep slopes. A thin cover of snow may occur at higher elevations. Small channels join the Suketi river in its upper reaches.

Its gradient abruptly changes once it enters the valley bottom. Thick deposits of boulders of various sizes are found on either sides of the water channel in the middle and lower courses of the Suketi river. The river has formed huge terraces, most of which are under cultivation.

Temperate and sub-tropical forests are found in the upper catchment of the Suketi river. The entire tract along the middle and lower courses of this river is being cultivated. Many human settlements have come up along the river Suketi, particularly in its lower course.

SUN KOSI RIVER

The Sun Kosi river is the largest tributary of the Kosi river system that drains eastern Nepal. It rises from a glacier on the southern slopes of the main Himalaya. Thereafter the Sun Kosi river flows for a considerable distance southwards to about 12 kms north of the Chatra gorge where all the three major tributaries of the Kosi river meet.

This river originates in a U-shaped glaciated valley. It is joined by a number of tributaries both in its glacial trough and along its course to its confluence with the other rivers of the Kosi system. These are--
-- a small snow-fed tributary joins the mainstream of the Sun Kosi river in its glacial trough
--- the Dudh Kosi draining the Mt. Everest area flows into the Sun Kosi river south of Okhar Dhunga
-- two small snow-fed tributaries from the northern flank of the Sun Kosi valley join the mainstream near Ramechhap.

A large part of the course of this river flows through a narrow, V-shaped valley. Thick forests are found in its catchment except in areas which are under a permanent cover of snow. A number of large settlements have come up along this river. These include Chautara and Ramechhap.

SUNDERDHUNGA RIVER

The Sunderdhunga river is a tributary of the Pindar river in the north-central part of the U.P. hills near the border of Garhwal and Kumaun. It rises as two mainstreams from the following glaciers--
-- the Sukhram glacier
-- the Panwali glacier which feeds the Panwali stream.

These two water channels merge to form the Sunderdhunga river in the Sunderdhunga meadows. Other snow-melt water channels joining this river are--
-- the Mrigthuni stream descending from the Mrigthuni glacier on the slopes of the peak bearing its name
-- the Mangtoli stream containing melt-waters of small hanging glaciers descending from the slopes of the Panwali doar and Bauljuri peaks
-- small tributaries drain into the Sunderdhunga river between the Sunderdhunga meadow and Dhungiadon.

In the upper and middle courses of this river the valley bottom is strewn with a thick deposit of fluvio-glacial sediments. Ground and terminal moraines are found near Dhungiadon which suggests that the glacier extended to this location in the past. The river descends very rapidly downstream of Dhungiadon and merges with the Pindar near Khati.

Moist alpine, sub-alpine and temperate forests are found in the Sunderdhunga catchment. Amongst the human settlements that have come up along this river are Dhungiadon and Jaloli.

SUPIN RIVER

The river Supin is one of the two main feeder channels of the Tons river in Garhwal. It rises from a valley glacier near the famous Har-ki-dun valley in Garhwal. Thereafter this river flows in a general direction towards south-west to merge with the Rupin at Naitwar and form the Tons river.

Har-ki-dun valley forms the upper catchment of this river. It is a large glacial amphitheatre hemmed by snow clad peaks of the main Himalaya from all sides. The snowy wastes of the valley glacier form the mainstream of the Supin river. This valley is the destination of hundreds of trekkers each year. The channel forms small islands as it winds its way along the wide valley bottom.

Thereafter the Supin river descends rapidly along a series of small waterfalls and rapids. It has carved a deep V-shaped valley across the lower hills of the main Himalaya.

Thick forests are found in the Supin catchment. These include alpine meadows in the Har-ki-dun area and sub-alpine and temperate forests in the middle and lower catchments. A number of small settlements have come up along this river. These include Har-ki-dun, Sandra and Naitwar.

SURU RIVER

The Suru river is a small tributary of the Shigar (south) river. It rises from the snowy wastes on the northern slopes of the main Himalayan range and merges with the Shigar (south) river after a short distance. Small snow-fed channels empty themselves into the Suru river at various places along its course.

The entire catchment of this river has been carved by the action of glaciers both ancient and present. In winters, snow covers a large part of the Suru valley and may lie on the ground till mid-May. The river channel may freeze in severe winters.

The valley bottom is strewn with striated boulders and moraines brought down by glaciers. Small hanging valleys open into the main valley. There is virtually no vegetative growth in the Suru catchment except for a very brief period in late summer when tufts of grass appear on the lateral and terminal moraines at lower elevations. Human habitation is very sparse though the Suru river lies along a trail across the Zaskar range which lie to the north.

TALUNG RIVER

The Talung river is a tributary of the Teesta river in northern Sikkim. It rises from the snout of the Talung glacier on the slopes of the Kanchanjunga massif. Thereafter this river flows along a U-shaped valley in a general direction towards south-east to join the Teesta river.

The upper tracts of the Talung valley are under a perpetual cover of snow. Small glaciers inside valleys pour their melt-waters into the mainstream of the Talung river. Glacial deposits are strewn all over the valley. The Talung river flows into the Teesta river a short distance after it emerges from its glacial trough.

Vegetation is restricted to alpine and sub-alpine meadows and scrub on the moraines. The Talung valley is visited by graziers in summer.

TAMUR RIVER

The Tamur river is the easternmost tributary of the Kosi system. It rises from the western slopes of the Kanchanjunga massif known as the Kumbhakaran Himal and the western flanks of the Singalila range near the border of Nepal and India.

There are two mainstreams of the Tamur river. Both are fed by glaciers. They have wide glacial troughs. These streams merge after about 2 kms downstream of which the Tamur flows towards south-west, turns towards south-east for a short distance before flowing along a south-westerly course to join the Sun Kosi and Arun rivers downstream of the small town of Dhankuta.

A large number of tributaries join the Tamur river in its upper tract. These are fed by glaciers on the southern and south-western slopes of the main Himalayan range.

The upper catchment of this river is under a cover of snow. Alpine, sub-alpine and temperate forests are found lower down the slope. Dhankuta is the largest settlement that has come up along the Tamur river.

TANG CHU RIVER

The Tang Chu river is the most important tributary of the Chamke Chu river. It flows into the latter a short distance upstream of the Chamke Chu-Dur Chu confluence after which the main channel is known as the Bumthang Chu river.

TANT GARI RIVER

The Tant Gari is one of the two feeder streams of the Ravi. It rises as small channels from the slopes of an offshoot of the Pir Panjal range in the area to the east of Bharmaur in Chamba district of Himachal Pradesh. The Tant Gari then quickly descends down the steep slopes to form the Ravi river after merging with the Bhadal river.

This river is fed by small glaciers or tongues of permanent deposits of snow that descend from the mountain slopes. The water melting from these deposits flows as small gravelly channels which merge to form the mainstream of the Tant Gari river. Small snow-fed tributaries join the Tant Gari river at various points all along its course.

The Tant Gari valley is U-shaped. Its bottom is strewn with boulders and morainic deposits laid down by glaciers in the past. Alpine, sub-alpine and temperate vegetation is found in this tract. There is no human habitation along the Tant Gari.

TAWANG RIVER

The Tawang river is a tributary of the Manas river. It rises from the snowy wastes on the south-facing slopes of the main Himalayan range in north-western Arunachal Pradesh. This river flows towards south to its glacial trough, turns towards south-west and flows into north-eastern Bhutan where it merges with the Manas river upstream of Tashi Gang.

The glacial trough of this river is U-shaped. The sides are lined with deposits of lateral moraines. The Tawang river flows along a narrow V-shaped valley in its middle and lower course. A tributary rising in Tibet merges with the mainstream a short distance upstream of Tawang. Another tributary originating in Tibet flows into the Tawang river near the border of Arunachal Pradesh and Bhutan. Smaller tributaries join this river from its left flank.

Dense forests occur in the catchment of the Tawang river. Alpine and sub-alpine vegetation covers the moraines and terraces in the upper tracts while temperate and sub-temperate forests are found at lower elevations. The famous Tawang monastery is situated high above the river bed near the mountain hamlet of Tawang.

TAWI RIVER

This is an important river draining the Jammu region of Jammu and Kashmir. The Tawi river rises on the southern slopes of the foothills of the Pir Panjal range. It is fed by springs emanating from underground water. In its upper reaches this river flows towards west, then takes a U-turn near Udhampur to flow in a southerly direction before attaining a south-westerly course near Jammu. The Tawi river enters the plains downstream of Jammu and flows into the Chenab river a short distance after crossing the Indo-Pak border.

The Tawi river flows along a V-shaped valley in its upper course. Thereafter it enters the Siwalik hills and the valley opens up. The river bed is very wide and strewn with sediments of all sizes that have been brought down by the river. The channel winds its way along this sediment-filled bed.

The river is very broad in Jammu just before it enters the plains. Terraces occur along the entire course of this river. Temperate forests are found in the upper tracts while dry sub-tropical and tropical riverine and thorn forests occur along the middle and lower courses of the Tawi river. The terraces in the foothills are under cultivation.

Jammu is the largest town through which the Tawi river flows. It also flows along a part of the foothill town of Udhampur.

TEESTA RIVER

The Teesta river system drains a part of the Darjeeling hills and the entire state of Sikkim. It rises from the Zemu glacier on the south-eastern slopes of the Kanchanjunga massif. Thereafter it flows towards east in its upper course, turns towards south-east and finally attains a southerly direction before entering the plains to the east of Siliguri. In the plains the Teesta river once again flows towards south-east and merges with the main channel of the Brahmaputra river in Bangladesh.

The Teesta river falls very sharply within a few kilometers of its origin at the tongue of the Zemu glacier lying at an elevation of over 4000 metres. It drops to an elevation of about 1000 metres near Singhik and Mangan in central Sikkim. This river flows along a very deep gorge which divides north Bengal or the hills of Darjeeling into two parts viz the Darjeeling-Tiger hill range in the west and the Kalimpong hills to the east.

This river is joined by many tributaries flowing in from different parts of Sikkim. These include--
-- the Lhonak river rising from the snowy wastes of northern Sikkim
-- the river Lachung which rises from Paunhri and joins the Teesta river at Chumthang
-- the Rangit river is a large tributary of the Teesta system. It is fed by glaciers on the southern slopes of the Kanchanjunga massif.

A permanent cover of snow occurs in the upper catchment of the Teesta river. Alpine, sub-alpine, temperate and sub-tropical moist forests are found at various altitudinal levels in the Teesta catchment. A number of human settlements have come up along this river. These include Chumthang, Lachen, Mangan and Teesta bridge.

TENGA RIVER

The Tenga river is an important tributary of the Kameng river which drains the western part of Arunachal Pradesh. It rises from the base of the offshoots of the main Himalayan range. Thereafter this river flows along a deep V-shaped valley to merge with the Kameng river near the town of Bomdila.

Thick forests cover the entire catchment of the Tenga river. These include sub-alpine, temperate and semi-evergreen forests. Small villages have come up all along the course of the Tenga river.

THI CHU RIVER

The Thi Chu river is the headwaters of the Raidak river in Bhutan. It rises from a glacier on the south-facing slopes of the main Himalaya. Thereafter it flows near the capital town of Thimpu and joins the Paro at Confluence downstream of which this river is known as Raidak.

TIRTHAN RIVER

The Tirthan river is a tributary of the Beas. It rises from the base of an offshoot of the great or main Himalayan range to the south-east of Kulu in Himachal Pradesh. Thereafter the Tirthan river follows a south-westerly course and flows into the Beas at Larji just before it cuts across the Dhauladhar range.

The feeder channel of the Tirthan is fed by deposits of ice almost all round the year. Some of its tributaries rise from aquifers and come out on the surface as springs.

The Tirthan flows along a deep V-shaped valley in its upper reaches. Lower down, the valley opens up and it is fairly wide near its confluence with the Beas river. The main geomorphic features of the Tirthan valley are incised meanders, river-built and river-cut terraces, cliffs and steep ridges.

The entire catchment of this river is covered by alpine, sub-alpine, temperate and sub-tropical coniferous and deciduous forests. Human habitation is in the form of small villages that exist along the river.

TONS RIVER

The Tons river is an important tributary of the Yamuna river. It rises as the following two feeder streams--
-- the Supin river rises in the northern part of the Tons catchment near the Himachal Pradesh-Uttar Pradesh border.
-- the Rupin river rises from a glacier at the head of the famous Har-ki-dun valley in the north-north-eastern part of the Tons catchment.

The two feeder streams merge near the mountain hamlet of Naitwar and the channel downstream of Naitwar is known as the Tons river. This river then flows for a considerable distance along the border of Himachal Pradesh and Uttar Pradesh before merging with the Yamuna river at Kals in the north-western part of the Dehradun valley.

The Tons river flows along a V-shaped valley. Its catchment bears some of the densest and richest forests in the western Himalaya. These are primarily birch, fir, spruce, blue pine, deoder, ban, kharsu and moru oak and chir pine forests. A number of settlements have come up along the Tons river. Amongst these are the hamlets of Naitwar, Tuni and Menus. (The latter was washed away in a devastating flash flood some years back).

TORSA RIVER

The river Torsa is also known as the Amo Chu. It drains western Bhutan. This river originates from a glacier in the Chumbi valley in Tibet. The Torsa river flows through a glaciated U-shaped valley across the Chumbi valley and enters Bhutan in its middle course.

In Bhutan the Torsa flows in a V-shaped valley. NW-SE-trending parallel offshoot ranges of the main Himalaya flank the river on either sides. The prominent geomorphic features include interlocking spurs, rock benches, cliffs, ridges and river terraces.

This river enters the lower hills in the Phuntsholing area. It has cut a gorge across the foothills and enters the plains along the Indo-Bhutan border. Thereafter the Torsa flows towards south-east and merges with the main channel of the Brahmaputra river in Bangladesh to the east of Rangpur.

A forest cover is found in the middle and lower courses of the Torsa river. The large terraces are under cultivation. Amongst the main settlements that have come up along this river are Sombe dzong and Phuntsholing.

TRISULI RIVER

The Trisuli river is an important eastern tributary of the Gandak system. It rises from the snow-fields of southern Tibet in the area to the south of Saka. Thereafter this river flows in a general direction towards south-east where it enters Nepal through a gorge across the central Himalayan axis. The Trisuli attains a southerly direction south of the Nepal-Tibet border and flows past interlocking spurs to turn towards west in its lower course. This river drains into the mainstream of the Gandak system about 75 kms downstream of Nuwakot.

A number of tributaries join the Trisuli river at different places.
-- a small tributary flowing in from the east joins the Trisuli river at Nuwakot.
-- the Burhi Gandaki river rising from southern Tibet flows into the Trisuli downstream of Nuwakot.

This river flows along a deep V-shaped valley that is hemmed by towering snow-clad mountains of the main Himalayan axis. The gradient is very steep in the tract upstream of Nuwakot. Small valley glaciers pour their melt-water into the Trisuli river in its upper course. Wide terraces occur in the lower valley.

Snow covers the upper catchment of the Trisuli river. Alpine pastures occur on the fluvio-glacial sediments at higher elevations. Sub-alpine birch and rhododendron and temperate coniferous and broad-leaved forests are found at various elevations. Nuwakot is the largest settlement that has come up in this tract.

The Indian government has constructed a large hydroelectric power station on the Trisuli river.

TSARAP CHU RIVER

The river Tsarap Chu is one of the feeder channels of the Zaskar river in Ladakh. It originates from the snows on the north-facing slopes of the main Himalaya near the border of Jammu and Kashmir and Himachal Pradesh. A number of snow-fed channels merge to form the Tsarap Chu river which in turn flows towards north-west to merge with the main channel of the Zaskar river at Padam.

The entire catchment of this river has been carved by the action of glaciers. Small glaciers occur in between the spurs of the main Himalaya and its offshoot ranges. Melt-waters emanating from these glaciers join to form the Tsarap Chu river. Thick deposits of moraines laid down by glaciers are found in the valley bottom.

There is a dearth of vegetative cover in this tract because of its position in the rain-shadow zone of the main Himalaya. Alpine and sub-alpine herbs appear for a very short season during the summer season. Some forms of vegetation may also be found in strips along channels of snow melt-waters.

The main settlements that have come up along this river are Char and Padam.

TSARI CHU RIVER

This is another name of the Subansiri river that drains central Arunachal Pradesh. It enters Indian territory as the Tsari Chu river. (For detailed description see 'Subansiri river').

UHL RIVER

The river Uhl is a tributary of the Beas river. It rises as two feeder channels in the area to the north of the Dhauladhar range in Himachal Pradesh. Thereafter the two channels cross this gigantic mountain barrier and merge at the base of the southern slopes to form the main channel of the Uhl river in Kangra area.

The river then flows for a considerable distance along the base of the Dhauladhar range. It turns towards south-east to merge with the Beas near the town of Mandi.

In its upper course the Uhl river flows along a deep V-shaped valley. The main channels have carved gorges across the Dhauladhar range. The valley opens up once this river enters the Kangra valley. The river bed is strewn with boulders of various sizes. Large river terraces occur along the lower course of the Uhl river. These comprise of a thick deposit of sediments brought down by it over the past thousands of years.

The upper and middle catchments of this river are covered by sub-tropical forests. The land along its lower course is under cultivation.

The hydel power house at Jogindernagar produces power from the waters of the Uhl river which are led through the mountain by means of a series of tunnels.

UJH RIVER

This river is a foothill river of the Jammu (Jasrota) area of Jammu and Kashmir. It rises as a small spring on the southern slopes of the lower Himalaya. Thereafter the Ujh river drains across the gently-sloping valley between the lower Himalaya in the north and the Siwalik hills in the south. It has cut a deep gorge across the Siwaliks before entering the plains of Punjab.

The lower Himalayan slopes which form the periphery of the upper catchment of this river are very steep. They are in the form of a series of ridges and saddles. Cliffs occur near the upper edge.

The Ujh river flows along a very steep gradient in its upper course. The water runs over small rapids before reaching the gentle slopes in the Jammu foothills. This river then begins to meander across the gently-sloping terrain. It has laid down huge terraces on either sides of the river bed.

Thereafter the Ujh river once again enters a V-shaped valley in its journey across the Siwalik hills which form a barrier across its lower course.

Sub-tropical dry forests are found in the Ujh catchment. There occur large patches of grasslands along the river bed. The terraces are under cultivation.

VASUKI GANGA RIVER

This is a small tributary of the Mandakini river in the Kedarnath valley of Garhwal. It rises from Vasuki tal which is a small glacial lake situated in the glacial trough lying to the east of the upper Mandakini valley.

This river descends rapidly along a U-shaped valley in its upper reaches and V-shaped gorge in its middle and lower course. Thereafter it merges with the Mandakini at Sonparyag.

The Vasuki Ganga river is primarily a high altitude channel whose mouth lies at an elevation of about 1700 metres. It descends over rapids and small waterfalls in its journey from Vasukital to Sonparyag. A number of small hanging valleys open into the main Vasuki Ganga valley at various places.

The upper catchment is devoid of a vegetative cover. Alpine meadows are found in moist shady depressions. Sub-alpine birch and rhododendron forests occur on glacial moraines. Temperate coniferous and broad-leaved forests are found at lower elevations. Human habitation is very sparse. Sonparyag is situated at the confluence of this river with the Mandakini.

WAKHA RIVER

The Wakha river is a tributary of the Shigar (south) river. It originates from the snowy wastes on the north-facing slopes of the main Himalaya in the Kargil area of Ladakh. This river then flows for a short distance before joining with the Shigar (south) river.

The entire valley of the Wakha river has been carved by the action of glaciers. Morainic deposits occur along the valley bottom. Vegetation is very poor and human population is sparse.

WONG CHU RIVER

The Wong Chu river is a tributary of the Raidak river in central Bhutan. It rises from the snowy wastes on the south-facing slopes of the main Himalaya. Thereafter it flows in a general direction towards south-south-east to join the Raidak.

Alpine pastures, and mixed conifer and broad-leaved forests are found in the catchment of the Wong Chu. Exposed, rocky areas also occur along this river. Glaciers and snow-fields cover its upper tracts.

YAMNE RIVER

The Yamne river is a large eastern bank tributary of the Dihang or Siang or Brahmaputra river in Arunachal Pradesh. It rises on the south-west slopes of the Abroka pass in north-central part of the state and flows in a general direction towards south to merge with the Brahmaputra river downstream of Silli.

This river has cut a V-shaped valley across the middle and lower Himalaya. Its entire catchment bears thick forests. Some of the large villages that have come up along this river are Dalbuing, Dumro, Sibhum and Silli.

YAMUNA RIVER

The Yamuna river is the largest tributary of the Ganga river. It drains western Garhwal and a part of eastern Himachal Pradesh. The mainstream of the Yamuna river rises from the Yamunotri glacier at the base of the Bandarpunch peak in the main Himalayan range of Uttarkashi district.

Thereafter the Yamuna river flows along a V-shaped valley in the general direction towards south-west to enter the plains downstream of Paonta town in Himachal Pradesh. In the plains this river flows past Haryana to Delhi and finally to the plains of Uttar Pradesh where it merges with the Ganga river at Allahabad.

The gradient of this river is very steep in its upper tract. The speed of the river gradually slows down as it nears the plains. Hanging valleys open into the river near Yamunotri. The river bed is strewn with striated boulders brought down by glaciers in the past. The river descends over a series of rapids. Morainic deposits are found along the sides of the upper Yamuna valley.

The Yamuna then flows along a valley whose flanks are formed by N-S-trending ridges. The main geomorphic features of the Yamuna valley are interlocking spurs, steep rock benches, gorges and terraces. The terraces have been formed by the river over the past thousands of years. Large terraces occur in its middle and lower coarses e.g. at Naugaon.

This river has cut a deep gorge across the NW-SE-trending Mussoorie ridge which is a part of the lower Himalaya near the mountain hamlet of Yamuna bridge. The river enters the dun valley near Kalsi. Another gorge has been cut by this river across the Siwalik hills downstream of Paonta town.

A number of tributaries drain into the Yamuna river. These have been discussed under 'Yamuna river system'.

Alpine, sub-alpine, temperate and sub-tropical vegetation covers the Yamuna catchment. These forests are degraded in some patches due to heavy biotic pressure. The main human settlements that have come up along this river are Yamunotri, Hanuman Chatti, Naugaon, Kalsi, Vikasnagar and Paonta.

The Yamuna river has been dammed at Dakpatthar to produce power and water for irrigation.

YAMUNA RIVER SYSTEM

The Yamuna river and its tributaries are a part of the Ganga catchment. The area drained by the Yamuna system extends from the Giri-Satluj water-divide in Himachal Pradesh to the Yamuna-Bhilangana water-divide in Garhwal. In fact the south-eastern slopes of the Shimla ridge are also drained by the Yamuna system.

The main rivers which constitute the Yamuna system are--

-- the mainstream of the river Yamuna which rises from the Yamunotri glacier
-- the river Tons which rises from the Har-ki-dun valley and joins the Yamuna near Kalsi
-- the Aglar river which rises at the base of the Yamuna-Bhagirathi water-divide, north-east of Chamba. It flows towards west to join the Yamuna at Yamuna bridge
-- the Giri river which rises in east-central Himachal Pradesh and merges with the Yamuna near Paonta
-- the Bata river is a small tributary of the Yamuna system. It drains the Kiarda dun (Paonta) valley and flows into the Yamuna downstream of Paonta
-- the Asan river draining the western part of the Dehradun valley. It flows into the Yamuna near Herbettpur.

YANG SANG CHHU RIVER

This is an eastern tributary of the Dihang or Siang or Brahmaputra in north-eastern Arunachal Pradesh. It rises as a small snow-fed channel from the western slopes of the water-divide between the catchments of the Dihang and Dibang or Siang rivers.

Many small snow-fed tributaries join this river as it flows between high snow-clad mountains towards north-west to join the Dihang or Siang river between Jidu and Tuting villages. The two large villages that have come up along this river are Nyering and Jidu.

YUMA CHHU RIVER

The Yuma Chhu river is a large tributary of the Subansiri river which in turn drains a large part of Arunachal Pradesh. This river rises in the snows of the main Himalayan range. Thereafter it flows towards south-west to merge with the Subansiri river.

This river flows along a deep V-shaped valley. The channel winds its way past interlocking spurs, rock benches and river terraces of different sizes which have been formed by the river over the past thousands of years. Steep ridges rise on either sides of the river.

Numerous small tributaries merge with the Yuma Chhu in its

course from the snows to its mouth. These are fed both by snow and by the spring emanating from the reservoir of underground water.

The entire catchment of the Yuma Chhu river is covered by dense forests. These range from alpine pastures at higher elevations to evergreen forests near its confluence with the Subansiri river. Numerous small human settlements have come up along this river.

ZASKAR RIVER

The Zaskar river is one of the largest tributaries of the river Indus in Ladakh. Its headwaters are known as the Tsarap Chu which originate from the snows on the north-facing slopes of the main Himalaya. These are joined by another feeder channel flowing in from the northwest and the Zaskar river is formed.

The entire catchment of the Zaskar river has been formed by the action of glaciers. Its valley is U-shaped and a number of hanging valleys open into the main valley of the Zaskar river.

Important tributaries of this river are--
-- the Tsarap Chu river rises from the north-facing slopes of the main Himalaya and joins the main river near Padam
-- the Doda is another snow-fed tributary of the Zaskar river
-- the Khurana river rises from the northern slopes of the Zaskar range and merges with the Zaskar river a little upstream of its confluence with the Indus river.

The Zaskar river has cut a deep gorge across the Zaskar range in its middle course. It flows into the Indus about 40 kms downstream of Leh.

The vegetative cover in the Zaskar catchment is confined to occasional tufts of grass on the moraines and small clumps of vegetation along channels formed by snow-melt waters. Human habitation is sparse. The main settlements that have come up along the Zaskar river are Abring and Padam.

Himalayan Lakes

BADANI TAL LAKE

This is a small lake set amidst steep slopes in the upper Lastar Gad river valley near Mayali in Garhwal. A series of faults caused by movements in the earth's crust have led to the formation of this lake. A fault has blocked the course of a stream draining this tract, thus creating the lake. Lower down the slope another fault has given rise to a smaller lake.

The slopes around Badani tal are covered with temperate forests. A large grassland occurs along its banks. There are small swamps and marshes around the periphery of this lake.

Ecological degradation has set in in the Badani tal lake due to the following factors:

a) Heavy inflow of silt from the adjoining areas.
b) Pollution by human beings and domestic cattle.

Its area is slowly decreasing as a result of these factors. The water has been rendered unfit for human consumption.

BEGNAS TAL LAKE

This is a small lake situated in the Pokhra valley of Nepal. It is a remnant of the vast lake that once covered the entire valley. There occur a number of swamps along the periphery of this lake together with laccustrine deposits of recent origin.

BHAGSUNATH LAKE

This lake is also known as Dal Lake. It is also located on the upper slopes of the Dhauladhar range in the Dharamshala area of Himachal Pradesh. It is fed by snow-melt waters from the surrounding areas.

Thick oak and conifer forests cover the catchment of this lake. Every year thousands of tourists visit the Bhagsunath lake. The once crystal clear waters are being polluted now.

BHIMTAL LAKE

The Bhimtal lake is the second largest lake in Kumaun. It is situated in the lower Himalaya in the area to the north-east of Haldwani. Bhimtal is a very beautiful lake that is visited by thousands of people each year. A small township has come up along the periphery of this lake. There is an island in the middle of the lake.

Geologists are of the opinion that the Bhimtal lake was created by a series of faults caused by movements in the earth's crust. Surface drainage was thus impeded and this led to the formation of the Bhimtal lake.

Thick forests cover the mountain sides around the Bhimtal lake. These include chir pine, ban oak and mixed deciduous forests. The climatic conditions vary from tropical to sub-tropical. Very heavy rainfall is experienced in this tract during the monsoon season.

The Bhimtal lake is undergoing retrogressive ecological changes due to the following causes:

a) *Sewage disposal*: A large quantity of sewage including human excreta is being emptied into the lake ecosystem.
b) *Sediment inflow*: Heavy biotic pressure on the surrounding forest and construction of roads and buildings has led to an increase in the sediment flowing into the Bhimtal lake.
c) *Tourists*: Thousands of tourists visit this lake each year. They pollute the water by disposal of wastes.

The problems brought about by these factors are--

-- the level of dissolved oxygen in the waters of this lake has dropped down to alarming levels. This is detrimental for the well-being of fresh-water fishes
-- the NO_3–N level in this lake goes upto about 350 mg per litre. This indicates that the Bhimtal lake is in a pre-eutrophication stage
-- pollution of the lake waters has led to the formation of certain poisonous substances on the lake bottom
-- there has been an increase in the fish mortality rate during the past 30 years
-- addition of organic matter reduces the drinking water quality due to various pathogenic micro-organisms directly or indirectly associated with the organic products and are responsible for a number of water-borne diseases in animal and human population.

CHANDRA NAHAN LAKE

This is a glacial lake in the main Himalaya to the north-west of Rohru in Himachal Pradesh. It lies at the origin of the Pabar river which is a tributary of the Tons river. The Chandra Nahan lake lies in a depression formed by the glacier that feeds the Pabar river.

High snowclad peaks surround this lake. It is fed by snow-melt waters. Alpine meadows grow on the banks of this lake in summer. Its waters are crystal clear and unpoluted.

CHANDRA TAL LAKE

This is a beautiful glacial lake located at the source of Chandra river in the Lahul valley of Himachal Pradesh. The towering main Himalaya hems the northern periphery of the Chandra tal lake. This lake is fed by meltwaters from the Chandra glacier.

The Chandra tal lake lies in a large depression formed by the glacier. Alpine vegetation grows on the surrounding moraines in summer. This lake freezes during the winter season. Its waters are crystal clear and free from pollution. A number of temples exist along the periphery of the lake.

CHANG CHENMO LAKE

This is a large brackish water lake in the Chang Chenmo area of north-western Ladakh. It is fed by a stream from the northern slopes of the Karakoram range. This lake is a brackish water-body and has no outlet. Smaller streams from the high mountains surrounding this lake drain into it. The Chang Chenmo lake freezes during the winter months.

CHHANGU LAKE

This is a small glacial lake in northern Sikkim near the road to the Nathu La pass. The Chhangu lake is fed by a glacial channel. It empties itself into a waterfall over a morainic plug into the valley below. There are many other small glaciated lakes in this tract. The water is crystal clear and unpolluted.

DAL LAKE

The Dal lake is one of the largest lakes in the Himalaya. It is situated in Srinagar within the famous Kashmir valley. In fact this lake is a major tourist attraction of Kashmir. This lake has an area of about 11.30 sq kms. Roads line the banks of the Dal lake. Small houseboats and shikaras are maintained by the local people in the waters of this lake. These are hired by tourists who flock to Kashmir from different parts of India and abroad.

The Dal lake is believed to be a remnant of a vast lake that once covered the entire valley. Floating islands are a characteristic feature of this lake. These are a mass of vegetation on which soil has been deposited for raising vegetables. Such floating islands are causing a severe strain on the ecology of the Dal lake.

Other causes responsible for the process of eutrophication that has begun to set in this lake are--
  (a) *Houseboats and shikaras*: Houseboats and shikaras disturb the lake's serene environment. Sewage from houseboats and hotels lining the lake is poured into its water, thus causing ecological degradation.
  (b) *Outwash*: Outwash from the agricultural fields around the lake, vegetable gardens and floating gardens that have come up both in and around the periphery of the lake are polluting the once crystal clear waters.
  (c) *Silt inflow*: In the recent past, the quantity of silt flowing into the lake waters has increased to alarming levels. According to an estimate, about 80 thousand tons of sediment is flowing into the Dal lake each year.

These factors have brought about the following adverse effects--
-- over the last 50 years the area of this lake has gone down from about 22 sq kms in 1940 to about 11.30 sq kms at present
-- the level of dissolved oxygen in the lake water falls down to about 4 mg per litre during the summer season which is the peak tourist season
-- the level of dissolved NO_3-N drops to about 7 mg per litre in summer
-- in recent years there has been heavy mortality of carp fish as breeding and spawning grounds lie along the periphery of this lake. These areas are the worst affected
-- there is profuse weed growth along the periphery of the Dal lake. This is to the tune of about 40 to 50 thousand tons each year. Weeds cause a retrogressive change in the lake's ecosystem
-- the sewage and outwash brings in about 16 tons of phosphorous and 365 tons of nitrogen into the lake waters each year
-- the habitat of zooplanktons and phytoplanktons too has been

adversely affected.

Nevertheless, the Dal lake remains one of the most beautiful lakes in the entire Himalayan region.

DEORI TAL LAKE

The Deorital lake is an enchanting body of water located in the mountains near Chopta in Chamoli district of Garhwal. It lies in the lower hills of the main Himalayan mountain wall. A depression formed by glacial movement in the past serves as a lake.

This lake is fed by a snow-melt stream. The runoff from the surrounding high mountains too drains into this lake. The slopes around Deorital are covered with dense coniferous forests. This lake can be approached after an arduous trek. Its waters are clear and unpolluted.

DODI TAL LAKE

This is a beautiful lake set amidst conifer-clad slopes in the main Himalaya near Uttarkashi in Garhwal. The Dodital lake lies in a depression forméd by ancient glaciation. It is fed by snow-melt waters flowing in from the surrounding high mountains.

Mixed coniferous forests dominated by deodar cover the steep slopes around this lake. Laccustrine deposits are found along its banks. Hundreds of trekkers visit this lake each year. It is reached after an arduous trek. The waters of this lake are clear and unpolluted.

GOHANA TAL LAKE

This was a small lake formed when a landslide blocked the flow of a tributary of the Alaknanda river system in Chamoli district of north-eastern Garhwal in the latter part of the last century. Gohana Tal lake became a famous tourist attraction. Heavy rains in July 1970 caused the natural dam to burst. This resulted in devastating flash floods in the entire Alaknanda valley causing wide-spread loss of life and property.

HEMKUND-LOKPAL LAKE

This is a famous lake located in the upper part of the Chamoli district in Garhwal. It is a large glacial lake lying on the cirque floor of the Saptsring glacier. It is fed by a stream from a hanging glacier located on the eastern slopes of the Saptsring peak. The Hemkund-Lokpal lake is surrounded by towering, snow-clad peaks of the main Himalaya.

Fluvio-glacial and laccustrine deposits are found along the periphery of this lake. Minor channels formed by snow-melt water from the surrounding slopes drain into this lake.

The Hemkund-Lokpal lake is the destination of thousands of Sikh pilgrims each year. A huge gurudwara stands on its banks. Guru Govind Singh is believed to have meditated on its shores. This lake is reached after an arduous trek from Govind Ghat on the road to Badrinath. Its waters are clear and unpolluted.

KAGBHUSAND TAL LAKE

This is a large glacial lake located on the slope of the Kankul Khal peak in north-eastern Chamoli in Garhwal. It is tenanted in a cirque of the Kankul Khal glacier which also acts as its feeder. This glacier feeds a mainstream of the Kagbhusand river which in turn drains into the Alaknanda river system.

The Kagbhusand tal is surrounded by snow-clad peaks of the main Himalaya. Alpine meadows occur along its banks. The waters of this lake are crystal clear and unpolluted.

KHAJIAR LAKE

The Khajiar lake is situated amidst beautiful deodar forests near Dalhousie in Chamba district of Himachal Pradesh. It lies in a depression formed by ancient glaciation. Dense conifer and broad-leaved forests cover the steep mountain slopes around this lake. The run-off from these slopes feeds the Khajiar lake.

This lake is the destination of hundreds of tourists each year. The grassy meadows surrounding it are under a severe strain due to human interference, horse riding and domestic cattle. Thus, the area of the Khajiar lake has shrunk to alarming levels in the recent past. Its periphery is surrounded by marshes and swamps.

KHURPA TAL LAKE

This is one of the many lakes of the Nainital area of Kumaun. It is situated near Nainital town and lies in a depression formed by movements in the earth's crust which blocked the flow of a small stream. Steep slopes covered with forests occur around this lake.

Ecological degradation has set in in this lake due to the following factors:
    a) Excessive inflow of sediments and sewage from the surrounding areas.

b) Pollution caused by the dumping of solid wastes into the water.

LINGZI TANG LAKE

This is a large lake in the Lingzi Tang region of north-western Ladakh near the border with Tibet. It is a brackish water lake that serves as an inland basin for snow-fed streams that surround it. A major feeder system flows in from the Karakoram range in the south.

The Salt lake is situated near this lake and it is believed that both these lakes were interconnected in the recent past. This lake freezes during the long winter season.

MANIMAHESH LAKE

This is an enchanting lake set amidst snow-clad peaks at an elevation of about 4200 metres in the Budhil valley near Bharmour in Chamba district of Himachal Pràdesh. In the backdrop lies the towering Kailash peak.

The Manimahesh lake lies in a glacial depression. It is fed by snow-melt waters from the surrounding slopes. Its waters are crystal clear and unpolluted.

MANSAROVAR LAKE

This is a very large lake situated in southern Tibet. High peaks including the Kailas or Kailash peak surround this lake which is revered by Hindus. Lord Shiva is believed to have meditated on its shores. A large depression formed by ancient ice ages serves to hold the water that pours in from the surrounding glaciers.

NAGIN LAKE

This is a small lake situated near Srinagar in the Kashmir valley. It is believed to be a remnant of the large Karewa lake that once covered the entire valley. The Nagin lake receives water from a number of snow-fed streams.

Marshes occur on the periphery of this lake. Small floating islands float on the lake waters. The Nagin lake is visited by thousands of tourists each year and this has led to the ecological degradation of its waters.

NAINITAL LAKE

The Nainital lake is situated in a large depression in Nainital town of Kumaun. The lake is surrounded by high peaks covered with chir pine and conifer forests. It is believed that this lake was formed due to faults produced by movements in the earth's crust. The lake is fed by streams bringing in fresh water from the mountain slopes.

The local people have divided this lake into two parts viz Mallital towards north and Tallital towards south. A road runs along the entire periphery of this lake. The temple of Naini Devi is situated on the banks of the Nainital Lake.

Thousands of tourists visit Nainital each year. They enjoy the serene beauty of this lake which is set amidst the lower Himalayan range. Boating and walking along the lake front is a popular mode of recreation with the tourists.

Ecological degradation has set in in the Nainital lake in the recent past due to the causes mentioned below:

a) *Sewage disposal*: A large quantity of sewage including human excreta is emptied into the Nainital lake. The quantity of sewage received by the lake waters is very high in summer due to the abrupt increase in the number of tourists staying at Nainital.

b) *Accelerated erosion*: Accelerated erosion on the slopes surrounding this lake has led to a drastic increase in the inflow of sediments being received by the Nainital lake. Construction of roads and hotels in the uplands has added to this problem.

c) *Boating*: Boating and sailing is very popular with the tourists. A rapidly increasing number of boats has resulted in disturbing the ecological balance of the lake waters.

Numerous ecological problems have beset the Nainital lake. These include--

-- the level of dissolved oxygen during the spring season is about 5 mg per litre. This falls to about 2.5 mg per litre in summer which is the peak tourist season. This condition has been considered to be very dangerous for fresh water-fishes.

-- the level of NO_3-N goes upto about 500 mg per litre which indicates an advanced stage of eutrophication

-- due to the disposal of sewage and other waste products into the Nainital lake, NH_3, H_2S, NO_3 and other toxic substances are formed at the bottom of this lake. This has an adverse effect on the physiology of the biotic organisms in the water body

-- there has been an increase in the fish mortality rate in the past 30 years. Each year a large number of fish perish in the Nainital lake

-- the spawning and breeding grounds of carp fishes are being destroyed by the sewage and excessive quantity of silt. The fishes of this lake breed in shallower waters near the periphery. It is near the periphery that the ecology has been disturbed to a large extent
-- addition of organic matter in water reduces the drinking water quality because of different pathogenic micro-organisms
-- excessive siltation has led to a decrease in the area of this lake.

NANDIKUND LAKE

This is a small lake on the southern slopes of the massive Choukhamba peak in Garhwal. The Nandikund lake is tenanted in an eastern cirque of this peak. The river Madhyamaheshwari rises from the Nandikund glacier and lake. This lake has been formed in a depression carved out by the glacier.

Very high mountains of the main Himalaya surround this lake. It is fed by snow-melt waters. Fluvio-glacial and laccustrine deposits are found along the periphery of this lake. Vegetative growth is virtually absent. This lake freezes in winter. Its waters are clear and unpolluted.

NAUKUCHIA TAL LAKE

This is a small lake in the Nainital area of Kumaun. It has been formed in a small depression due to geological movements in the earth's crust. Heavy inflow of sediments from the surrounding mountain slopes has endangered the very existence of this lake.

PANGONG TSO LAKE

This is a brackish water lake on the Indo-Tibet border in the area to the south-east of Shyok in Ladakh. The Pangong lake receives water from numerous snow-fed streams draining the surrounding snow-covered slopes. The famous Khurnak fort near the international border stands on the banks of this lake. This lake freezes in winter.

PHEWA TAL LAKE

This is the largest of the three lakes situated in the famous Pokhra valley of Nepal. It has a length of about 5 kms. The Phewa tal lake is fed by a snow-fed river. The town of Pokhra has come up around this lake.

It is believed that in the past the entire Pokhra valley was submerged by a lake which drained away when the natural dam burst.

Phewa tal is the largest remnant of this lake.

Laccustrine deposits of recent origin are found all along the periphery of the lake. Boulders of varying sizes are embedded in the soft lake deposits.

The Phewa tal is visited by thousands of tourists of each year. Many hotels have come up along the lake front. Ecological degradation of this lake is being brought about by the following factors:

    a) *Siltation and sewage*: In the recent past the quantity of silt and sewage flowing into this lake has increased abruptly due to the degradation of the uplands and population pressure.

    b) *Pollution*: The lake water is being polluted by the dumping of solid wastes into it.

PHUSMDO LAKE

The Phusmdo lake is situated in the trans-Himalayan tract of Mustang Bhot in northern Nepal. It has been formed in a glacial depression. This lake is fed by a tributary of the Kali Gandaki river.

High snow-clad mountains surround the Phusmdo lake. The surface runoff from these slopes flows into the lake. Alpine and sub-alpine forests cover its catchment and banks.

The waters are crystal clear and unpolluted by human interference.

RENUKA LAKE

This is an oval lake located near Dadhau in the lower Himalaya of Sirmaur in Himachal Pradesh. It lies in a depression formed by a fault in the earth's crust. The Renuka lake is fed by a small stream flowing in from the lower Himalayan hills that surround it. These slopes are covered with dense sub-tropical forests.

A temple of Renukaji exists along the banks of this lake. Thousands of tourists and pilgrims visit the Renuka lake each year. Ecological degradation has set in due to the vast quantity of sediments that flow into this water body from the degraded uplands each year.

REWALSAR LAKE

The famous Rewalsar lake is located near Mandi in central Himachal Pradesh. This lake is fed by small mountain streams. High mountains of the middle Himalaya surround this lake. The surface runoff from these slopes flows into the Rewalsar lake. A number of floating islands float on the water's surface. This lake occurs in a depression formed either by moving ice in the past or a fault due to movements in the earth's crust. Dense forests occur on the slopes around this lake. There are many temples on the banks of the Rewalsar lake.

RUPAKOT TAL LAKE

This is a small lake situated in the Pokhra valley in Nepal. It is a remnant of the vast body of water that covered the entire valley in the past. It is fed by the snow-fed runoff from the surrounding high mountains.

RUPKUND LAKE

This is a large glacial lake on the slopes of the main Himalaya in north-eastern Chamoli in Garhwal. It came into prominence when the mysterious remains of frozen human beings were found on its banks. Rupkund lake is fed by a glacier. Vegetation is absent. This lake freezes during the winter season. Its waters are crystal clear and unpolluted.

SAGERIYA TAL LAKE

This is a small lake near Nainital in Kumaun. Its depression has been formed by a fault. In the recent past ecological degradation has set in due to heavy sedimentation and pollution. This has altered the ecosystem of this lake.

SALT LAKE

This is a large brackish water lake in the Aksai Chin region of Ladakh near the Indo-Tibet border. The Salt lake receives water from the snow-clad mountains that surround this tract. A large river flows into this lake from the southern face of the Karakoram range in the north.

It is believed that this lake is a remnant of the sea that once covered the Tibetan plateau. A number of smaller salt lakes occur near the main lake in Aksai Chin. This lake freezes during the long winter months.

SANASAR LAKE

This is a beautiful lake situated at an elevation of about 2000 metres near the mountain hamlet of Patni top in Udhampur district of Jammu and Kashmir. It lies on the slopes of the lower Himalayan mountain range.

The Sanasar lake is fed by a small channel. Deodar forests cover the mountain slopes around this water-body. However, the lake is fast turning into a marsh due to the growth of weeds and excessive siltation.

The following causes are responsibl;e for the eutrophication of the Sanasar lake—
  a) Grazing and other forms of biotic pressure on the forests of the surrounding slopes have resulted in a sharp increase in the level of silt flowing into the water.
  b) Growth of weeds due to interference with the lake's fragile ecosystem.

The Jammu and Kashmir government has taken up an ambitious project to save this lake from extinction.

SHASTRU TAL LAKES

This is a collective name given to a group of lakes in the amphitheatre of the Khatling glacier in the Ghansali area of Garhwal. These lakes lie below the Shastru peak and hence the name. They have formed in depressions carved out by the Khatling glacier and its feeders.

Snow-covered peaks surround the Shastru tal lakes. The meltwaters from these slopes drain into the lakes. Vegetation is virtually absent in this tract. These lakes are reached after an arduous trek from Ghuttu. Their waters are unpolluted.

SHESHNAG LAKE

This is a famous lake on the ancient pilgrim route to Amarnath. It is located in the area to the north of Pahalgam on the slopes of the main Himalayan range in the Kashmir valley.

The Sheshnag lake has formed in a glacial depression. It is surrounded by snowclad peaks from which water flows into it. This lake is also fed by an adjoining glacier. Alpine meadows come up around this lake in late summer. The Sheshnag lake is an important halting place for pilgrims to and from Amarnath.

This lake freezes in winter. Its waters are crystal clear and unpolluted.

SPANGGUR TSO LAKE

This is a small lake on the Indo-Tibetan border near the Pangong Tso in the area to the south-east of Shyok in Ladakh. It receives water from the snow-covered mountains that surround it. This is primarily a brackish water lake with virtually no outlet. This Spanggur Tso lake freezes in winter.

SUKHA TAL LAKE

This is one of the many lakes that occur in the Nainital area of Kumaun. It is situated near Nainital town. This lake lies in a depression formed by a fault. In the past it contained water all around the year but heavy sediment inflow from the adjoining slopes has virtually filled up this lake and hence the name Sukha "dry" tal. At present there is water in this lake only during the rainy season.

TSO LHAMO LAKE

This is a beautiful glacial lake in northern Sikkim in the upper catchment of the Teesta river. It lies in a depression formed by moving ice. Snow-clad mountains surround the Tso Lhamo lake. Its waters are clear and unpolluted.

TSO MORARI LAKE

The famous Tso Morari lake is located in the Rupshu area of Ladakh between the Zaskar range in the south and the Ladakh range in the north. Towering peaks having elevations of over 6500 metres surround this lake on all sides. Amongst these is the Chalung and Kyungzing La peaks.

The Tso Morari lake lies in a vast glacial depression. It serves as an inland drainage basin for the snow-melt waters that flow into it from different directions. It has no outlet and hence its water is brackish. The banks are lined with thick deposits of tethyan sediments. This lake freezes in winter.

VASUKI TAL LAKE

This is a small glacial lake tenanted in the glacial trough lying to the east of the Chor Bamak glacier which is near the source of the Mandakini river in Garhwal. The Vasuki Ganga river rises from this lake.

Towering snow-clad peaks surround this lake on all sides. The melt-water from these slopes drains into the Vasuki tal lake. It is also fed by the Vasuki glacier. There is virtually no vegetation in this tract.

This lake freezes in winter. Its waters are crystal clear and unpolluted.

WULAR LAKE

This is a large lake located to the north-west of Srinagar in Kashmir valley. It is the largest fresh-water lake in the Himalaya. Geologists are of the opinion that the Wular lake is a remnant of a large body of water that once covered the entire Kashmir valley. This has been referred to as the Karewa lake and was formed when the river Jhelum was blocked by the rising Himalayan range. Later on the Jhelum broke through this natural barrier and the Karewa lake drained away thus leaving a number of lakes and marshes in the Kashmir valley. The Wular lake is the largest such remnant.

A number of small snow-fed streams drain into the Wular lake. These flow in from different directions, both from the Pir Panjal range in the south and the main Himalaya in the north.

The Wular lake is visited by thousands of tourists each year who go there for water sports. Ecological degradation of this lake is being brought about by the following causes:

a) *Sediment and sewage inflow*: A large quantity of sediment and sewage is flowing into the lake waters each year from the surrounding areas.
b) *Water sports*: Water sports like boating, sailing and water skiing are disturbing the fragile ecosystem of this lake. Tourists also dump waste products into the water.

Himalayan Glaciers

ANNAPURNA GLACIER

This glacier is tenanted in an amphitheatre on the middle slopes of the Annapurna massif that forms a part of the main Himalayan range of north-central Nepal. The melt-water from this glacier flows into the Gandak river system.

The Annapurna glacier is fed by smaller tributary glaciers in side valleys. They form icefalls at the junction with the trunk glacier. There occur thick deposits of fluvio-glacial sediments at various places in the area vacated by this glacier.

Vegetative cover is by and large absent. This glacier can be approached via Pokhra and Nuwakot in central Nepal.

API GLACIER

The Api glacier is situated on the middle slopes of the Api peak that occurs on the main Himalaya near the north-western border of Nepal with Kumaun. The melt-water from this glacier flows into the Kali river system that drains western Nepal.

This glacier descends down along a relatively steep slope. It is fed by tributary glaciers in side valleys and depressions. Virtually no vegetation grows in this tract. The Api glacier can be approached via Vaitadi in western Nepal.

ARU GLACIER

The Aru glacier is located on the southern slopes of the main Himalaya in Kashmir. The trunk glacier is tenanted in a trough. It feeds the Aru river which is a tributary of the Liddar river.

Small hanging valley glaciers open into the trunk glacier. The Aru glacier has receded considerably in the recent past. Moraines cover the valley bottom. Alpine and sub-alpine vegetation comes up in this tract from late summer to mid-autumn. The Aru glacier can be approached via Pahalgam in Kashmir.

BAGANI GLACIER

This is a small glacier situated on the lower slopes of the Nanda Devi massif in U.P. Himalaya. Its snow-melt waters flow into the Rishiganga river.

BALTORO GLACIER

The Baltoro glacier is situated on the southern slopes of the central Karakoram range in Baltistan area of Jammu and Kashmir. It is tenanted in a huge amphitheatre that is hemmed by high peaks. This glacier gives rise to the Shigar river which is a tributary of the river Indus. Its length is about 62 kms. Thus it is the second largest glacier in the Himalaya.

Large tributary glaciers feed the main Baltoro glacier. These include--
-- a glacier from the south-western slope of the Gasherbrum peak
-- a tributary glacier from the north-western slope of the Masherbrum peak.

The trough of this glacier is very wide. Its central part is a vast snow-field. Small valley glaciers form icefalls where they meet the trunk glacier. The side walls vary from very steep to precipitous. The Baltoro glacier has carved striations on the surrounding country rocks. Moving ice has formed depressions which serve as basins for numerous glacial lakes. The Baltoro glacier can be approached via Skardu in Ladakh.

BANKUND GLACIER

The Bankund glacier is situated in north-western Garhwal. It lies in a huge amphitheatre on the south-facing slopes of the main Himalayan range. A horse-shoe shaped jagged ridge encircles this trough from three sides. Many snow-clad towering peaks including the Rataban and Deoban peaks form a part of this ridge.

Numerous small tributary glaciers feed the trunk glacier. These include--
-- two glaciers from the slopes of the Rataban and Nilgiri peaks in the south
-- three glaciers from the slopes of the Deoban peak in the west
-- small hanging glaciers from the slopes of the Kagbhusand peak facing north.

The Amrit Ganga river rises from the snout of the Bankund glacier. The floor of the glacial trough of the trunk glacier contains extensive layers of ground moraine overlain by steps of terminal moraine and ridges of lateral moraine. The glacier consists of ice and rocky wastes. It has carved a wide trough. The side slopes vary from very steep to precipitous. Scree deposits are found along the flanks of the glacial trough.

The Bankund glacier expands rapidly in winter. Avalanches roll down the side slopes of its valley. The temperature remains below the freezing point for long periods. Bulk of the total annual precipitation is in the form of snow.

BARA SHIGRI GLACIER

This is the largest glacier of the Lahul valley of Himachal Pradesh. It is tenanted in a cirque on the middle slopes of the main Himalayan range. Small tributary glaciers feed the trunk glacier. High mountains surround this glacier on three sides.

The melt-water from this glacier flows into the Chenab river. The entire tract is devoid of a vegetative cover.

BARMA GLACIER

The Barma glacier is tenanted in a cirque located to the west of the Kalpani glacier in northern Chamoli in Garhwal. It has a length of about 0.75 kms. The Barma Gad river rises from this glacier.

A number of smaller glaciers feed the main glacier. These are located in side hanging valleys. Extremely cold conditions prevail in this tract. The snow-melt channels freeze during the long winter months. Grassy meadows have come up on the thick deposits of moraines that occur at various places in the glacial trough.

BARMAL GLACIER

The Barmal glacier is situated in the north-western part of Chamoli district in Garhwal. It is a hanging glacier tenanted in the cirque of the Barmal peak. The Hom Gadhera river rises from the snout of this glacier. It drains into the Pushpawati river.

The glacial amphitheatre is surrounded by high peaks. Moist alpine and temperate vegetation occurs in this tract. This glacier can be approached via Gobindghat in Chamoli district.

BARUN GLACIER

The Barun glacier is located in a hanging valley on the southern slopes of the Makalu peak that forms a part of the main Himalayan range of north-eastern Nepal. The Barun river rises from the snout of this glacier and flows into the Kosi river system.

Towering peaks including the Makalu, which is the fourth highest peak in the world surround the Barun glacier valley from three sides. Numerous glaciers in side valleys feed the trunk glacier. These form icefalls where they open into the main glacial valley.

Ancient deposits of lateral and terminal moraines are seen at various places in this valley. Moving ice has carved pot holes in which water accumulates. Huge boulders have been displaced by this glacier. They lie near its snout. The melt-water flows away as many braided channels before merging to form the main stream of the Barun river. This glacier can be approached via Bhojpur in eastern Nepal.

BEAS KUND GLACIER

The Beas Kund glacier lies on the south-facing slopes of the towering Pir Panjal range near the famous Rohtang pass in Manali area of Himachal Pradesh. It gives rise to the mainstream of the Beas river.

This glacier is tenanted in a cirque on the upper slope not very far from the summit of the high peaks of the Pir Panjal range. The meltwaters from this glacier are joined by numerous streams draining away from minor deposits of ice in depressions before forming the mainstream of the Beas river.

The Beas Kund glacier is of a relatively smaller size as compared to the longer glaciers that feed the large rivers in other parts of the Himalaya. Deposits of varying sizes are found along the sides and at the snout of this glacier.

Alpine and sub-alpine meadows come up in the cirque of this glacier in summer. The Beas Kund glacier is visited by graziers in late summer. This glacier can be approached via Manali in Kulu district.

BHADAL GLACIER

The Bhadal glacier is situated on the south-western slopes of the Pir Panjal range in the Bara Banghal area of Himachal Pradesh. The melt-waters from this glacier give rise to the Bhadal river which acts as the mainstream of the Ravi river.

This glacier lies in a typical amphitheatre that is surrounded by soaring snow-clad peaks on all sides. Minor tributary glaciers feed the trunk glacier. These are tenanted in moist shady depressions on the lower and side slopes of the main glacial valley.

The surface of this glacier is strewn with boulders and other glacial deposits. Moraines occur along its sides and near the snout. The Bhadal glacier has carved striations on the surface of its valley bottom. The snowmelt water flows away from the snout in the form of numerous braided channels that merge downstream to give rise to the Bhadal river.

Heavy snowfall in winter causes a rapid expansion of this glacier. Alpine and sub-alpine meadows cover the moraines from late summer to autumn. This glacier is visited by migratory graziers in the hot season.

BHAGA GLACIER

The Bhaga glacier is tenanted in an amphitheatre on the slopes of the main Himalayan range in the Lahul area of Himachal Pradesh. It gives rise to the Bhaga river which merges with the Chandra river to form the Chandra-Bhaga or Chenab river.

High, snow-clad peaks surround this glacier on all sides. It has carved small depressions and pot holes on the valley bottom. Moraines occur along the flanks and at the tongue of this glacier.

Alpine pastures come up in the amphitheatre of this glacier in late summer. These are visited by migratory graziers. This glacier can be approached via Koksar and Tandi in Lahul-Spiti district.

BHAGIRATHI KHARAK GLACIER

This glacier is tenanted in a cirque on the southern slopes of the main Himalayan range in the area to the east of Kedarnath in Garhwal. The channel draining away from this glacier forms the Mandakini glacier.

BHRIGUPANTH GLACIER

The Bhrigupanth glacier is located on the south-facing slopes of the main Himalaya, north of Uttarkashi in Garhwal. It descends from a cirque on the south-eastern slope of the Chaukhamba massif. This glacier is primarily a feeder of the Gangotri glacier. The tributary glacier lies to the east of the trunk glacier.

Small deposits of ice in hanging valleys open into the trough of the Bhrigupanth glacier. Icefalls join this glacier at various places. The valley bottom is gently sloping. Moving ice has formed striations on the surrounding country rocks. Moraines occur sporadically in the glacial trough. The side walls are steeply sloping.

A thick deposit of ice covers the entire trough during the winter season. It descends very fast with the onset of summer.

BIAFO GLACIER

The Biafo glacier is located on the south-facing slopes of the Karakoram range in the Baltistan area of Ladakh. It has a length of about 60 kms and descends from a large glacial trough. The mainstream originating from this glacier flows into the Shigar river which in turn is a tributary of the Indus river. Small valley glaciers feed the trunk glacier at various points.

There is virtually no vegetative cover in this tract. The Biafo glacier can be approached via Skardu in Ladakh.

BICHOM GLACIER

The Bichom glacier lies in north-western Arunachal Pradesh. It is tenanted in an amphitheatre and gives rise to the Bichom river which in turn drains into the Kameng river system.

BURH GLACIER

The Burh glacier is located on the lower slopes of the Nanda Devi massif along the border of Garhwal and Kumaun. It has a length of about 3 kms. The Panwali river rises from this glacier. This river is a tributary of the Sunderdhunga river which in turn drains into the Alaknanda river system.

Small tributaries join the Burh glacier. These are—
-- glaciers in hanging valleys descending down from the slopes of the Panwali doar and Bauljuri peaks
-- small glaciers descending down from the Mangtoli peak.

A huge quantity of fluvio-glacial sediments is found on the floor of the glacial trough. The channel formed by the snow-melt water displays a braided pattern. The layer of old ground moraine is thick. The glacial trough narrows down to an epigenetic gorge about 3 kms downstream of the snout of the Burh glacier.

Avalanches are common, particularly in winter. Alpine grasses come up on the moraines in late summer and die in late autumn. This glacier can be approached via Karanparyag in Chamoli district.

BURLA GLACIER

This is a small glacier located in a hanging valley on the western slopes surrounding the Pindari glacier in the U.P. Hiamalya. It is a tributary of the main glacier.

CHANDANWARI GLACIER

The Chandanwari glacier is located on the south-facing slopes of the main Himalayan range in Kashmir valley. It is tenanted in a trough at the base of the Pissoo Top pass along the pilgrim route to Amarnath. The Liddar river, a tributary of the Jhelum rises from the snout of this glacier.

This glacier is small in extent. It has receded rapidly in the recent past. Alpine and sub-alpine meadows come up in summer in the areas vacated by the melting snow. The Chandanwari glacier can be approached via Pahalgam in Kashmir.

CHANDRA GLACIER

The Chandra glacier is located on the slopes of the main Himalaya in the Lahul-Spiti district of Himachal Pradesh. It gives rise to the Chandra river which joins with the Bhaga river to form the Chenab.

This glacier is tenanted in a cirque of the towering peak. Small tributary glaciers join the trunk glacier. Thick deposits of moraines are found in this tract.

The Chandra tal lake lies in a depression formed by the Chandra glacier. This glacier can be approached via Koksar in Lahul-Spiti district.

CHANDRA NAHAN GLACIER

This glacier is situated in a small amphitheatre on the southeastern slopes of the main Himalaya in the area to the north-west of Rohru in Himachal Pradesh. The melt-water from this glacier forms the mainstream of the Pabar river which in turn flows into the Tons river.

Towering peaks having elevations of over 6,000 metres encircle this glacier. The main body of ice bears both recent and old glacial debris which includes huge boulders. The Chandra Nahan glacier has formed striations on the valley floor.

Minor tributary glaciers join the trunk glacier. It has carved a depression and in it lies the Chandra Nahan lake which is fed by the melt-water from the snout of this glacier. Smaller depressions of similar nature are found elsewhere in this tract.

Alpine and sub-alpine meadows and scrubs come up in the amphitheatre of this glacier from late summer to mid-autumn. It is visited by migratory graziers. This glacier can be approached via

Rohru in Shimla district.

CHANGA BANG GLACIER

This is a small glacier located on the slopes of the Nanda Devi massif in U.P. Himalaya. Its melt-waters drain into the Rishiganga river.

CHANGME KHANGPU GLACIER

This glacier is tenanted on the south-facing slopes of the main Himalayan range in northern Sikkim. Its melt-waters flow into the Teesta river system. The Changme Khangpu glacier has receded drastically during the recent past.

CHATURANGI GLACIER

The Chaturangi glacier is situated in the south-facing slopes of the main Himalaya of north-central Garhwal. It is tenanted in a cirque on the lower slope of the Chaukhamba massif. The Chaturangi glacier is a western tributary of the Gangotri glacier.

This glacier lies in a U-shaped trough. Numerous hanging valleys open into this trough on both sides. Terminal and lateral moraines are found where this glacier meets the trunk Gangotri glacier. The Chaturangi glacier can be approached via Gangotri in Uttarkashi district.

CHO OYU GLACIER

This is a small glacier tenanted on the middle slopes of the Cho Oyu peak which is a part of the main Himalayan range of north-eastern Nepal. One of the two mainstreams which merge to form the Bhola Kosi river originate from the snout of this glacier.

Fluvio-glacial sediments cover the icy surface of the Cho Oyu glacier. Towering peaks occur in the backdrop. Vegetation is virtually absent in this tract. This glacier can be approached via Okhar Dhunga in east-central Nepal.

CHOMOLHARI GLACIER

The Chomolhari glacier is situated on the middle slopes of a peak of that name in north-western Bhutan near the border with Tibet. The melt-water from this glacier flows into the Raidak river system draining western Bhutan. This glacier has a length of about 3 kms.

Moraines and other fluvio-glacial sediments of recent and ancient origin are found along this glacier. The Chomolhari glacier has receded by about 200 metres in the recent past. This glacier can be approached via Chukha and Confluence in western Bhutan.

CHONG KUMDAN GLACIER

The Chong Kumdan glacier is situated on the lower slopes of the Karakoram range. It is tenanted in a trough that is surrounded on all sides by high peaks. The melt-water from this glacier flows into the Shyok river which in turn joins the river Indus.

The Chong Kumdan glacier had blocked the flow of the Shyok river several times in the past. Thus the Gapshan lake was formed which drained away once the ice dam gave way. This glacier can be approached via Skardu in Ladakh.

CHOR BAMAK GLACIER

The Chor Bamak glacier is located in the north-western part of Chamoli district in Garhwal. It lies on the lower slopes of the Kedarnath peak. Many glacial troughs open into the main Chor Bamak glacier. Each of these troughs terminate into a huge cirque with high snow-clad peaks in the background.

The Mandakini river rises from this glacier. The mainstream flows in a braided channel pattern near the snout of the glacier. A huge terminal moraine occurs near the famous Kedarnath temple. The snout of the glacier lies lower than the crest of the terminal moraine.

The bottom of the glacial trough is wide. Steep walls extend virtually right upto the valley bottom. Hanging valleys open into the main glacial trough. Huge boulders occur with thick deposit of ice. This glacier expands in winter due to very heavy snowfall. Alpine meadows cover lateral and terminal moraines. This glacier can be reached via Sonparyag, Gaurikund and Kedarnath in Chamoli district.

GANGOTRI GLACIER

This is a large glacier located in the northern tract of Uttarkashi district in Garhwal. It has a length of about 26 kms. The snow-fields of the Gangotri and its tributary glaciers are enclosed by a horse-shoe-shaped ridge dotted with numerous high-rising peaks which include the Kedarnath, Satopanth and Mana Parbat.

The main tributary glaciers which feeds the Gangotri glacier are--
-- the Manda, Bhrigupanth, Meru and Kirti Bamak glaciers in the east

— the Chaturangi and Raktravarna glaciers in the west.

The glacial trough of this glacier is over 4 kms wide. It is strewn with boulders and moraines. Hanging valleys open into the main glacier at various places. The Gangotri glacier has receded by about 0.6 kms in the last 50 years. Very heavy snowfall is received in this tract in the winter season and the glacier expands.

The Bhagirathi river rises from the snout of this glacier. Its origin is known as Gaumukh. Small meadows are found in the glacial trough. These include Nandanvan which is located 2 kms upstream of Gaumukh. This glacier can be approached from Harsil and Gangotri in Uttarkashi district.

GASHERBRUM GLACIER

The Gasherbrum glacier is located on the southern slopes of the Karakoram range in the Baltistan area of Ladakh. It lies at the base of the Gasherbrum peak. This glacier has a length of about 26 kms. The melt-water from this glacier joins the Shyok river system. Glaciers in hanging valleys open into the trunk glacier.

No vegetation grows in this tract due to the extreme conditions of cold. This glacier can be approached via Skardu in Ladakh.

GAURI SHANKAR GLACIER

The Gauri Shankar glacier is located at the base of a peak of that name on the main Himalayan range of north-eastern Nepal. The melt-water from the snout of this glacier forms the mainstream of the Bhola Kosi river which in turn flows into the Kosi river system.

This is a relatively small glacier situated in a cirque. Small deposits of ice in depressions feed the trunk glacier. The cirque floor is littered with fluvio-glacial deposits. The Gauri Shankar glacier can be approached via Okhal Dhunga in central Nepal.

GORA GLACIER

This is a small glacier tenanted on the south-facing slopes of the main Himalayan range of Himachal Pradesh. This glacier has receded in the recent past due to a negative mass balance.

HISPAR GLACIER

The Hispar glacier is situated in the southern slopes of the Karakoram range in the Baltistan area of Ladakh. This is a very large glacier feeding the mainstream of the Shigar river which in turn drains into the river Indus. The trunk glacier has a length of about 60 kms. Thus, this is the third largest glacier in the Himalayan region.

The large tributary glaciers which feed the Hispar glacier are--
-- valley glaciers from the northern slopes of the Haramosh massif
-- valley glaciers from the south-facing slopes of the Kanjut Sar massif.

Numerous glaciers of smaller extent join the trunk glacier on both sides of the amphitheatre in which it is tenanted. The central portion of this glacier is a vast snow-field while its sides contain debris eroded by the huge body of moving ice.

The entire tract is devoid of a vegetative cover. The Hispar glacier can be approached via Skardu in Ladakh.

KAFNI GLACIER

Kafni glacier is situated on the south-western slopes of the Nanda Devi massif along the border of Garhwal and Kumaun. It gives rise to the Kafni river which is a tributary of the Pindar river that in turn flows into the Alaknanda river system.

Two main tributary glaciers feed the Kafni glacier. These are--
--a valley glacier on the eastern flank of its glacial trough
--a small glacier on the western slope of its glacial trough.

The Kafni glacier is about 2.5 kms in length though its trough has a length of about 5 kms. Its width is about 1 km in the upper portion. This glacier has receded by about 2 kms in the recent past.

High mountain ranges encircles the Kafni trough on two sides. Its side walls are very steep and bear small glaciers in hanging valleys. The crest of the terminal moraine is at a relatively lower level. A huge quantity of debris and fluvio-glacial sediment is found on the valley floor.

The melt-water forms a braided channel on the valley bottom. Alpine and sub-alpine grasses come up in the trough from late summer to mid-autumn. This glacier can be approached via Gwaldam in Almora district.

KAGBHUSAND GLACIER

This glacier is located in the northern part of Chamoli district in Garhwal. Numerous snow-clad pyramidal peaks enclose the trough of this glacier. In the east are the Gauri Parbat, Dhanesh Parbat and Hathi Parbat peaks; in the south is the Barmal peak and smaller peaks on an offshoot spur of the Gauri Parbat peak lie in the north. The Kagbhusand glacier has a length of about 4 kms. Snow-melt waters from this glacier merge with into Bhyundar river.

The tributary glaciers which feed the trunk glacier are—
--glaciers from the Dhanesh Parbat and Oti-ka-Danda in the east
--glaciers from the Kankul Khal peak in the west.

This glacier has shown a significant level of recession in the recent past. Lateral moraines are very evident in the trunk and tributary glaciers. A thick deposit of ground moraine, glacial till and other fluvo-glacial material is found on the entire valley floor and also as mounds and cones on either flanks of the trough.

Alpine and sub-alpine meadows cover the moraines in the glacial trough. Steep to precipitous slopes extend to the base of the valley bottom. The snow-melt water has formed braided channels in the trough. Small pot holes have been carved on the valley floor by moving ice. The Kagbhusand glacier can be approached via Gobindghat in Chamoli district.

KALPANI GLACIER

The Kalpani glacier is situated in the northern part of Chamoli district in Garhwal. It is tenanted in the cirque of Vishnudhar massif which in turn is a part of the main Himalayan range. This glacier has a length of about 5 kms.

The trough of the Kalpani glacier is not very wide having a maximum width of about 1 km. There are virtually no hanging valleys opening into the main glacial trough. The side walls of its valleys are very steep and extend right upto the trough bottom.

The snow-field of this glacier is strewn with boulders of various sizes. There occur lateral and old terminal moraines at various places. Alpine meadows have come up on them. A number of small waterbodies are found in the depressions formed by moving ice.

The Kalpani glacier is the source of the Dudhganga river which is also known as the Kalpani Gad. Many small channels of snow-melt water merge to form the main channel of this river.

KAMET GLACIER

This glacier is tenanted on the middle slopes of the Kamet massif in north-western Garhwal. It consists of the main glacier and its eastern boundary known as the Eastern Kamet glacier. The melt-waters from this glacier flow into the Pushpawati glacier.

KANCHANJUNGA GLACIER

The Kanchanjunga glacier lies on the south-eastern slopes of the Kanchanjunga peak in north-western Sikkim. It occupies a hanging valley near the valley of the Zemu glacier. This glacier has a length of about 16 kms. The melt-water from its snout flows into the Teesta river system draining Sikkim.

Tributary glaciers feed the trunk glacier. No vegetation grows in this tract. The Kanchanjunga glacier can be approached via Singhik and Mangan in central and north-central Sikkim.

KANGCHEDA GLACIER

The Kangcheda glacier is situated at the base of the main Himalayan range in northern Bhutan. It is tenanted in a cirque that is surrounded on three sides by towering peaks.

Numerous small tributary glaciers feed the trunk glacier. No vegetative growth occurs in this tract.

KANGTO GLACIER

The Kangto glacier is located in a U-shaped valley at the base of the Kangto group of peaks in the main Himalayan range of north-western Arunachal Pradesh near the border with Tibet. The mainstream of the Kameng river rises from the snout of this glacier.

This glacier has a length of about 1 km. It has vacated a considerable part of its valley in the recent past. The Kangto glacier can be approached via Bomdila in south-western Arunachal Pradesh.

KANKUL KHAL GLACIER

The Kankul Khal glacier is situated in the north-western part of Chamoli district in Garhwal. It lies on the lower slopes of the Kankul Khal ridge in a cirque. This glacier is a tributary of the Kagbhusand glacier and serves as its western feeder.

The snow-melt waters from the Kankul Khal glacier feed the Kagbhusand river which in turn is a part of the Pushpawati river system. Small glaciers and permanent deposits of moving ice are located in the side valleys of the glacial trough. Icefalls from these hanging valleys feed the Kankul Khal glacier.

The valley bottom is littered with sediments of all sizes. Channels formed by the melting snow meander between these fluvio-glacial wastes and merge to form a single channel. Avalanches are common particularly during the winter season.

Alpine meadows have come up on the mounds formed by the lateral and terminal moraines and also on the glacial till along the side slopes. This glacier can be approached via Gobindghat in Chamoli district.

KHATLING GLACIER

The Khatling glacier is situated in the northern part of Tehri district of Garhwal. It lies on the lower slopes of the Bhartekuntha peak which is a part of the main Himalayan mountain wall. The total length of this glacier is about 1.5 kms.

Small tributary glaciers in side valleys open into the main trough of the Khatling glacier. They have formed U-shaped valleys. A number of small lakes occur in the depressions formed by moving ice. These lakes freeze in winter when the temperature in the entire tract remains below the freezing point for a long period. Bulk of the total annual precipitation is in the form of snow.

The Bhilangana river rises from the snout of the Khatling glacier. Numerous channels of snow-melt water merge to form the mainstream of this river.

The bottom of the glacial trough is littered with glacial sediments. Alpine meadows have come up on moraines both within the main valley and in the side valleys. The Khatling glacier can be approached via Ghamsali and Ghuttu in Tehri district.

KHUMBU GLACIER

This is a famous glacier situated on the south-western slopes of the Everest massif in north-eastern Nepal. The trunk glacier has a length of over 5 kms. It lies just below CWM amphitheatre on the traditional route to Mount Everest with the highest mountain peak in the world towering in the backdrop. The melt-water from this glacier flows into the Kosi river system. Other peaks which surround this glacial amphitheatre are Lhotse and Nuptse.

The Khumbu glacier lies in a wide U-shaped valley having a gently sloping bottom. Small tributary glaciers in hanging valleys join the trunk glacier at various places. Lateral and terminal moraines are found along the sides and at the snout of this glacier. Old fluvio-glacial deposits also occur along the valley bottom usually in the form of mounds or boulders of different sizes. Small depressions formed by the moving ice contain water that freezes in winter.

The entire tract is devoid of any form of vegetation. This glacier is visited by most expeditions to Mount Everest. It can be approached via Namche Bazar in north-eastern Nepal.

KIRTI BAMAK GLACIER

The Kirti Bamak glacier is located on the south-facing slopes of the main Himalaya of north-central Garhwal. It is an eastern feeder of the Gangotri glacier. The trough is U-shaped with its bottom having a gentle slope towards east and south-east. High snow-clad peaks of the Chaukhamba massif encircle the Kirti Bamak trough. Small hanging valleys open into this glacier.

Vegetation is virtually absent in this tract as it lies above the snow line. The Kirti Bamak glacier can be approached via Gangotri in Uttarkashi district.

LAL MATI GLACIER

The Lal Mati glacier is located at the head of the Mandal valley in Chamoli district of Garhwal. It lies on the lower slopes of the Lal Mati peak which in turn is a part of the main Himalayan range. This glacier is about 0.7 kms long.

The glacial trough is U-shaped but narrow. There occur extensive moraines and other fluvo-glacial deposits. Side hanging valleys open into the main glacial trough. The Lal Mati glacier gives rise to the Balkhila river. It is approached via Mandal in Chamoli district.

LUNANA GLACIER

The Lunana glacier is tenanted in a U-shaped valley at the base of the main Himalayan range in northern Bhutan. It has a length of about 2 kms and the valley extends to an elevation as low as 4150 metres. A large tract has been vacated by the receding glacier in the recent past. The valley is strewn with fluvio-glacial sediments.

MACHHUPUCHHARE GLACIER

This glacier is situated at the base of the Machhupuchhare peak or Fish-tail mountain which is a part of the main Himalaya of north-central Nepal. It gives rise to the mainstream of the Seti Gandak river which in turn drains into the Gandak river system.

The Machhupuchhare massif towers over this glacier. Small deposits of permanent snow in depressions feed the trunk glacier. This tract is almost entirely devoid of a vegetative cover. This glacier can be approached via Pokhara in central Nepal.

MANDA GLACIER

The Manda glacier is located on the south-facing slopes of the main Himalaya in north-central Garhwal. It is primarily a feeder or tributary glacier of the Gangotri glacier. High mountain peaks surround this glacier on all sides. Its trough is littered with glacial sediments.

Glacial till and scree is found on the side slopes of the glacial trough. Avalanches occur in winter. The temperature remains below the freezing point for long periods each year. Vegetation is virtually absent in this tract as it lies above the snowline.

MASANG KANG GLACIER

The Masang Kang glacier lies at the base of the main Himalayan range in northern Bhutan near the border with Tibet. It has a length of about 2 kms. The trunk glacier is fed by a number of tributary bodies of ice in side valleys. Vegetation is virtually absent in the valley of the Masang Kang glacier.

MERU GLACIER

The Meru glacier is located on the lower slopes of the main Himalayan range in the area to the north of Uttarkashi in Garhwal. This river of ice is tenanted in a cirque on the south-eastern slope of the massive Chaukhamba ridge. The Meru glacier is a tributary or feeder glacier of the Gangotri glacier. It lies to the east of the trunk glacier.

The floor of the glacial trough has a gentle slope towards the Gangotri glacier. Minor hanging valley glaciers open into the Meru glacier. The sides of its trough have a steep to precipitous slope. Glacial till occurs along its flanks.

The glacial trough is largely devoid of a vegetative cover as the entire tract lies above the line of perpetual snow.

MILAM GLACIER

The Milam glacier is located on the south-facing slopes of the main Himalayan range in the north-western Garhwal. It descends from the slopes of the ridge connecting the towering Kohli and Trisuli peaks. The Milam river rises from the snout of this glacier. It flows into the Alaknanda river system.

Many small glaciers tenanted in side valleys serve as feeders to the trunk glacier. The valley bottom is littered with fluvio-glacial sediments. The Milam glacier has shown a significant level of recession in the recent past.

MRIGTHUNI GLACIER

The Mrigthuni glacier is located on the lower slopes of the Nanda Devi massif along the northern border of Garhwal and Kumaun. It has a length of about 6 kms and is tenanted in a cirque on the slopes of the Mrigthuni peak. The Sukhram river rises from the snout of this river. It is a tributary of the Sunderdhunga river.

This glacier has carved a trough whose bottom has a gentle slope. It is strewn with thick deposits of fluvo-glacial sediments. Steep to precipitous slopes extend almost upto the valley bottom. Numerous valley glaciers on either flanks of this trough feed the trunk glacier.

The glacial trough is known as the Sukhram trough. Alpine and sub-alpine meadows and scrubs come up on the moraines from midsummer to late autumn. A thick blanket of snow covers the entire tract in winter.

MUSTANG GLACIER

This glacier is situated in the trans-Himalayan tract of Manang Bhot in north-central Nepal near the border with Tibet. It occupies an amphitheatre on the southern slopes of the towering Lo massif. The Kali Gandaki river rises from the snout of this glacier.

A number of minor tributary glaciers join the trunk glacier. These are tenanted in hanging valleys. No vegetation grows in this tract as it lies across the main Himalayan range. This glacier can be approached via Pokhra and Beni in central Nepal.

NANDA DEVI NORTH GLACIER

It is a small glacier located on the slopes of the Nanda Devi massif along the border of Garhwal and Kumaun. Its melt-waters drain into the Rishiganga river.

NEHNAR GLACIER

It is a small glacier tenanted on the snow-covered slopes of the main Himalayan range in Kashmir. This glacier has receded during the past 50 years or so due to a negative mass balance.

NITI GLACIER

This is a small glacier situated on the southern slopes of the Niti pass in Garhwal. It lies on the main Himalayan range and marks the border of Garhwal and Tibet. The Dhauliganga river rises from this glacier and flows into the Alaknanda river system.

A number of hanging glaciers open into the trunk glacier. The Niti glacier expands rapidly in winter. The Dhauliganga river rises in the form of small channels which merge to form the mainstream. This glacier can be approached via Badrinath in Chamoli district.

NUBRA GLACIER

The Nubra glacier is located on the southern slopes of the Karakoram range in Ladakh region of Jammu and Kashmir. It is a large glacier tenanted in a huge amphitheatre that is ringed by towering peaks. This glacier gives rise to the Nubra river which in turn flows into the Shyok river.

Large tributary glaciers open into the trunk glacier. These include--
-- valley glaciers from the north-western slopes of the Sasser La massif
-- valley glaciers tenanted in cirques on the south-eastern slopes of the Karakoram range.

Small glaciers in hanging valleys feed the Nubra glacier. They occur on all sides of the glacial amphitheatre. The central part of this glacier is in the form of a vast snow-field. Lateral moraines are found along the flanks and at the junction of the tributary glaciers with the trunk glacier.

No vegetation grows in this tract as it lies above the snow level and due to the extreme conditions of cold. This glacier can be approached via Leh in Ladakh.

PANWALI GLACIER

The Panwali glacier is tenanted on the south-facing slopes of the main Himalaya in north-western Garhwal. The melt-water from this glacier is one of the feeder streams of the Sunderdhunga river.

PHOKSUMDO GLACIER

The Phoksumdo glacier is situated on the south-eastern slopes of the Kanjiroba range in the trans-Himalayan tract of north-central Nepal near the border with Tibet. It gives rise to the mainstream of the river Phoksumdo which is a tributary of the Bheri river.

This glacier is tenanted in a cirque that is surrounded by towering peaks. It is strewn with both ancient and recent fluvo-glacial sediments. No vegetation occurs in this tract. The Phoksumdo glacier can be approached via Beni and Tarakot in north-central Nepal.

PINDARI GLACIER

This is a large glacier situated near the northern boundary of Garhwal and Kumaun. It is tenanted in a huge amphitheatre formed by high peaks amongst which the most prominent is the Nanda Kot. The Pindari glacier gives rise to the Pindar river which is a part of the Alaknanda river system.

The Pindari glacier gathers snow from three feeder glaciers. These are—
— a large glacier from the slopes of the Nanda Kot peak in the north-west
— the Burla glacier in a hanging valley on the western slopes
— a smaller glacier from the east.

This glacier is located in a wide trough. Its floor consists of a large expanse of undulating ground with widely spread ground moraines and old terminal moraines. The eastern flank of the glacial trough is very steep and many small hanging valley glaciers are tenanted on the fretted ridge.

The trough narrows down near the snout of the glacier. In this section the floor has a large number of moraine steps overlain by glacial till. The western slope is relatively gentler in the upper tracts but becomes steeper lower down.

The Pindari glacier has retreated by about 3.2 kms in the past 150 years. It has left behind a vast wasteland consisting of boulders and recently laid down fluvo-glacial sediments. The glacier quickly expands soon after the arrival of winter snow.

Alpine and sub-alpine meadows are found near the snout of this glacier from mid-summer to late autumn. This glacier can be approached via Gwaldam and Khati in Almora district.

PURBI KAMET GLACIER

The Purbi or east Kamet glacier is situated on the higher Himalaya of north-western Garhwal. It is tenanted in a cirque on the south-eastern slopes of the Kamet massif. The stream draining away the melt-waters from this glacier acts as a feeder to the Kamet river which in turn forms a part of the Alaknanda river system.

The glacial trough is surrounded by high peaks on three sides.

Avalanches roll down the steep slopes in winter. Alpine meadows have come up on the moraines in the trough of this glacier.

RAIKANA GLACIER

The Raikana glacier is located on the south-facing slopes of the main Himalaya of north-western Garhwal. It descends down from a cirque on the Kamet massif. The snow-melt stream from this glacier is one of the three channels that merge to form the Kamet river which in turn flows into the Alaknanda river system.

Small glaciers in side valleys open into the trunk glacier. Glacial till and moraines occur on the valley bottom. Alpine meadows have come up on the mounds in the glacial trough.

RAKAPOSHI GLACIER

This glacier is located on the lower slopes of the Karakoram range in the Gilgit area of Ladakh. It is tenanted on the north facing slopes of the Rakaposhi massif. The Rakaposhi glacier feeds an eastern tributary of the Hunza river which in turn flows into the river Indus.

The Rakaposhi glacier lies in a trough whose bottom has a gentle slope towards north and north-west. Boulders and rocks are strewn all over the surface. This glacier can be approached via Gilgit in Ladakh region of Jammu and Kashmir.

RAKTRAVARNA GLACIER

The Raktravarna glacier is situated in north-central Garhwal. It is tenanted in a cirque on the lower slopes of the Chaukhamba massif which is a part of the main Himalayan range. This glacier is a western feeder of the Gangotri glacier.

The trough is U-shaped. High peaks encircle this glacier on three sides. The valley sides bear thick fluvio-glacial deposits. The side walls are very steep.

The Raktravarna glacier can be approached via Gangotri in Uttarkashi district.

SALTORO GLACIER

The Saltoro glacier is located on the southern slopes of the Karakoram range in Ladakh. It is tenanted in a cirque of the Saltoro massif. This glacier feeds one of the two mainstream of the Saltoro river which in turn drains into the Shyok river.

Numerous tributary glaciers feed the trunk glacier. These descend from the hanging valleys on either flanks of the main glacial trough. Icefalls formed by smaller glaciers open into the main valley.

Mounds of terminal and lateral moraines occur along the lower part of the glacier. Moraines have also been deposited at the junction of the tributary glaciers with the trunk glacier. Other fluvio-glacial sediments are found along the flanks of this glacier.

The Saltoro glacier has formed striations on the country rocks. Small depressions on the valley floor are filled with water. There is virtually no vegetative growth in this area. The Saltoro glacier can be approached via Khapalu in Ladakh.

RAMANI GLACIER

It is a small glacier in the upper Rishiganga catchment of Chamoli district in Garhwal.

RATABAN GLACIER

This glacier is located at the base of the Rataban peak in north-western Garhwal. It is a tributary glacier of the Tipra glacier.

RISHI GLACIER

This is a small glacier tenanted on the slopes of the Nanda Devi massif in U.P. Himalaya. The headwaters of the Rishiganga river rise from this glacier.

SATOPANTH GLACIER

This glacier is located in the Kedarnath area of Garhwal. The channel formed by its melt-waters is one of the feeder channels of the Mandakini glacier.

SIACHEN GLACIER

The Siachen glacier lies in the extreme north-central part of Jammu and Kashmir near the border of India and Tibet. It has a length of about 72 kms and is the largest glacier in the world outside the polar regions. The Siachen glacier is located on the north-facing slopes of the Karakoram range. It feeds the Mutzgah or Shaksgam rivers that flows parallel to the Karakoram range before entering into Tibet.

Large tributary glaciers open into the main glacier from both sides of its trough. The trunk glacier and its tributaries are in the form of a vast icefield particularly during the winter season when continuous snowfall is received for several weeks at a stretch.

The Siachen glacier lies in a vast trough whose width is more than 2 kms. The sides of the glacier are strewn with rocks and boulders. The glacier has carved characterisitc striations on the country rocks. However, the central part of this glacier is a vast snow-field.

Numerous icefalls have been formed at the junction of small valley glaciers with the trunk glacier. Lateral moraines occur at the confluence of larger tributary glaciers with the trunk glacier. The side walls of the glacial trough are steeply sloping. Avalanches roll down these slopes quite often particularly in winter.

This glacier encompasses a vast tract in winter. There are virtually no signs of recession. This tract is more or less devoid of a vegetative cover both due to its high elevation and latitude. Bulk of the total annual precipitation is in the form of snow.

The Siachen glacier can be approached via Skardu in Ladakh.

SOLA KHUMBU GLACIER

This glacier is located on the southern slopes of the Everest massif on the main Himalayan range of north-eastern Nepal. It lies in a side valley of the main Khumbu glacier. The stream draining away the melt-water from this glacier joins the Kosi river system.

The Sola Khumbu glacier occupies a large amphitheatre on which stands the Thyangboche monastery on a huge platform made up of morainic material. This body of ice has formed striations on the bed rocks. There occur thick deposits of fluvio-glacial sediments on the valley bottom.

Alpine vegetation comes up on the mounds of moraines in summer. This glacier may be approached via Namche Bazar in north-central Nepal.

SUKHRAM GLACIER

This is a small glacier tenanted on the southern slopes of the main Himalaya in north-western Garhwal. It feeds the Sunderdhunga river.

TALUNG GLACIER

The Talung glacier is located at the base of the Talung peak which is an extension of the Kanchanjunga massif in north-western Sikkim. The melt-water from this glacier gives rise to the Talung river which in turn flows into the Teesta river system. The Talung glacier can be approached via Singhik in central Sikkim.

TAMUR GLACIER

The Tamur glacier lies on the south-western slopes of the Kanchanjunga massif on the border of Nepal with Sikkim. It gives rise to the Tamur river which is the easternmost tributary of the Kosi river system.

This glacier is tenanted in a hanging valley with the Kanchanjunga group of peaks known as the Kumbhakaran Himal in the backdrop. It is fed by smaller tributary glaciers in side valleys. This glacier can be approached via Dhankuta in eastern Nepal.

TIPRA GLACIER

The Tipra glacier is situated at the head of the famous Valley of Flowers in Garhwal. It has a length of more than 5 kms though the glacial trough is upto 8 kms long. The glacial trough is encircled by many high peaks, viz Rataban and Gauri in the east, Mukat and Nar Parbat in the north and Saptsring in the south.

The tributary glaciers which feed the Tipra glacier include
-- the Rataban glacier from the base of the Rataban peak
-- the Gauri glacier from the base of the Gauri peak
-- other small valley glaciers.

The Tipra river feeds the Pushpawati or Bhyunder river that flows through the Valley of Flowers. The floor of the glacial trough is overlain by thick cover of ground morainic and fluvio-glacial deposits of recent origin.

The temperature remains below the freezing point for long periods in winter. A vast quantity of glacial till and accentuating undulations on the valley floor have been deposited by avalanches particularly during the cold season. Bulk of the total annual precipitation is in the form of snow. Alpine and sub-alpine meadows occur on the moraines.

The Tipra glacier can be approached via Gobindghat and Ghagaria in Chamoli district.

TRISUL GLACIER

This is a small valley glacier in the upper Rishiganga catchment of Garhwal.

UMASI GLACIER

The Umasi glacier is located on the northern slopes of the main Himalayan range in Ladakh region of Jammu and Kashmir. It gives rise to a mainstream of the Zaskar river which in turn flows into the Indus river. This glacier is tenanted in a cirque of the Umasi La peak.

This glacier is elongated in shape. The upper and lower portions are narrow while its central part is very broad. Small valley glaciers open into the trunk glacier. The Umasi glacier can be approached via Leh in Ladakh region.

UTTARI PAIKANA GLACIER

The Uttari Paikana glacier is located in the northern part of Garhwal. It rises from the southern slopes of the main Himalayan range. This glacier is tenanted in a cirque of the towering Kamet massif. A large icy stream rises from the snout of this glacier. It acts as a feeder to the Kamet river which flows into the Alaknanda river system.

Large scree slopes descend down from the high mountains. The valley floor contains a thick deposit of fluvio-glacial sediments. Avalanches roll down the slopes frequently during the winter months.

VASUKI GLACIER

This is a small glacier located near the source of the Mandakini river in Garhwal. It feeds the Vasuki Ganga river. The melt-waters of this glacier form a part of the Mandakini river system.

ZEMU GLACIER

The Zemu glacier is situated in a large U-shaped valley at the base of the Kanchanjunga massif in north-western Sikkim. It has a length of about 26 kms and is the largest and the most famous glacier of the eastern Himalaya. The Teesta river rises from the snout of this glacier.

Many tributary glaciers feed the trunk glacier. The side valleys in which these glaciers lie open into the main Zemu valley from different directions. Icefalls and waterfalls have formed at the junction of the tributary glaciers with the Zemu glacier.

High peaks including the Kanchanjunga and Jonsang lie in the backdrop of this glacier. There occur thick morainic deposits at various places indicating the position of the snout of the glacier at different periods. It is believed to be retreating in the recent years.

The Lachen Gompha monastery lies near the snout of the Zemu glacier. This glacier can be approached via Gangtok, Singhik and Mangan in south-central and north-central Sikkim respectively.